*Labor Industry Relations
in the Early Twentieth Century:
An Autobiography*

Labor Industry Relations in the Early Twentieth Century: An Autobiography

STEWART SCRIMSHAW

Labor Industry Relations in the Early Twentieth Century:
An Autobiography

Thanks to Allan Stern for valuable assistance in preparing this book for publication.

The Troy Book Makers
Troy, New York
www.thetroybookmakers.com

Printed in the United States of America

To order additional copies of this title, visit www.tbmbooks.com

ISBN: 978-1-61468-023-9

Contents

Foreword

by Herbert G. Zollitsch

Rarely does one find the experience and accomplishment of an academic person so versatile as that of the author of this volume. A native of England, he emigrated to this country at the age of 19 years. Prior to that time, he had mastered a skilled trade through 5 years of apprenticeship. While at night school, he studied art, building construction and drawing. This occupation proved to be the means of securing higher education in his beloved America.

His experiences with industrial relations are significant since the author was on the ground floor, so to speak, as industrial relations had its beginning during the first years of the twentieth century.

Dr. Scrimshaw's career has covered many facets. He was the first administrator of the first modern apprenticeship statute of modern times, and that in the progressive state of Wisconsin. He is the author of a book on apprenticeship.

He was a Personnel Director of a large industrial organization; Director of the cooperative relations of a pioneering university engineering cooperative program; a Professor of Economics; Director of the Milwaukee Regional Labor Board under the National Relations Labor Board (NLRB); public panel member of the Chicago Regional War Labor Board, and a mediator and arbitrator in many labor disputes over a long stretch of years.

In a period in excess of 40 years, he has been a Professor of Economics and Industrial Relations at Marquette University.

Part of that time he was Associate Dean of the College of Business Administration, and the Director of the Evening Division.

Dr. Scrimshaw has given of his time and energy for many local public services. For many years he has been a much-sought-out speaker and lecturer before local and national organizations, and a career-long student of industrial relations both here and abroad.

Dr. Scrimshaw's experiences with the development of industrial relations is of special interest since it covers a unique period of our history, a period of the greatest dynamism of all time, reaching from the "horse and buggy" days to the jet age. His account is an interesting presentation of a record which his colleagues have induced him to write. They believe that it will prove informative and interesting to all managerial personnel of modern industry and commerce, as well as to all students of industrial relations and labor economics.

Herbert G. Zollitsch
Professor and Chairman
Industrial Management Department
Marquette University
Milwaukee, Wisconsin
May 9, 1968

Introduction

by Stewart Scrimshaw

In presenting the following record I have been motivated by two principal considerations: First, to give something of a unique personal record for the benefit of any who may be interested, and second, to relate some interesting experiences with the development of industrial relations that can only be known to one who has been a participant in the industrial arena.

Visiting manufacturing plants immediately prior to the Great War of 1914-1918 (as we called it then), it was plain to see that the only type of industrial organization was on military lines. Authority was communicated through the "line" of command – first the President, then the works manager, the general foremen, the department foremen and finally the individual employees. Unions had no standing with industrial employers before the war. Mutual relationship as understood in the concept of "Industrial Relations" did not begin to develop until the pressures of the War, as related in Chapter VI. In fact, what was involved in the term "industrial relations" was not properly understood until the early 1920s.

It is axiomatic that there is no such thing as a purely objective analysis of human behavior situations. Our points of view arise out of what we are or have become. It seems fitting to me, therefore, that in the recital of evolvement in this socio-economic phenomenon of developing industrial relations, something should be incorporated that reveals a measure of the character and personality of the author.

With this in mind, I have especially devoted the first two chapters to my earlier personal development and early experience. This should help to shed light on many factors which conditioned me for what was to be my role in later years.

The other chapters treat different facets in the field of industrial relations dealing with industrial education, protective legislation, labor relations, labor law and administration, and personnel management. Then there is a chapter on some career highlights. The final chapter—entitled "Retrospect" —is the *pot pourri* of reflections which come only in the philosophic years.

These observations necessarily give many behind-the-scenes episodes which, when viewed in retrospect, may seem almost incredible as they did to my students when related in class. The period covered dates from the beginning of the twentieth century to the decade of the 1960s.

Stewart S. Scrimshaw
Wauwatosa, Wisconsin
May, 1968

Chapter I

ANTECEDENTS OF A CAREER

Nothing Ventured, Nothing Gained

At the age of 14 years I had exhausted the educational opportunities furnished by the local public schools in England. At that time and place, high school studies were available only in a private school in the town of Boston, England, ten miles away, which was expensive and in general a school tending to create "snobs." My father was not in a position to provide higher education for all the members of the family, so it seemed to me that the family resources should be employed in furnishing higher educational opportunities for the girls of the family, and that the boys should make their own way.

With this in mind, I was determined to learn a trade and use it to obtain the means to continue my education. One August day of the year 1901 I was tending the family horse, which furnished the means for transportation in those days. As the horse grazed on the rich roadside grass, while I was lying on my back fascinated with the ascent of the warbling skylark, my younger brother brought me the daily paper so that I could read the advertisements. In this paper was an advertisement for an apprentice to learn bricklaying, plastering, site setting, etc. It excited me.

I answered this advertisement without consulting parental authority. It brought a favorable response. My father gave consent for me to be apprenticed, if that was what I wanted. This meant leaving home to live ten miles away, which in those days seemed a great distance.

I was formally apprenticed for five years. This apprenticeship is referred to elsewhere in these memoirs. It was completed on August 8, 1905.

I was tempted many times to "jump" my apprenticeship contract. However, I was conditioned by the family tradition of integrity which was the compelling factor in causing me to fulfill my apprenticeship. At the conclusion, my "master," as the employer was named in the contract, gave me a bonus of two pounds sterling. This was traditional. It seemed like a big sum but at the time it amounted to about three weeks wages. I left the firm at this time and went on my own.

The following months I worked for my father, repairing brickwork on our home and other property which we owned, and undertook special masonry jobs for neighbors. However, my main task at this point was to prepare for an examination to qualify for a certificate in Building Construction, a subject which I had been studying in night school during the apprenticeship. This coveted certificate from the National Board of Education, I achieved.

This constituted the first step of what became a long and interesting career. I really believe that I got a greater thrill in obtaining that particular certificate than I experienced years later in obtaining my college diploma. England at that time had only a few universities and these were mainly devoted to purely academic curricula. However, it should be said here that it has rarely been understood in this country how much opportunity was afforded in England for high grade continuation learning through evening schools, correspondence schools, and the like, even as early as the 1900's.

The year 1906 was a memorable one. The unpopular Boer war in South Africa had ended, and a general election for members of

Parliament took place. The election turned out the Conservative government responsible for the war and established the opposition Liberal party in power. This new government ushered in an era of many far-reaching reforms that could well be described as the British "new deal." It was an exciting time and one which furnished great intellectual stimulation. I was now really thirsting for knowledge. Although I attended evening school three evenings a week from 7:30 to 9:00 p.m., I was not satisfied with my educational progress.

Early in the year I got the suggestion that I could make faster progress in educational development if I went to America. Therefore, I made my decision to come to the United States. I came to the United States because I had learned it was practicable to earn one's way through college, and because there would be little or none of the social snobbery of a clan society which tends to discountenance the efforts of a non-privileged person earning his way through college. "America" was the magic word in those days. Building mechanics were in demand and well-paid. I soon made up my mind that I would go to America. However, at that time, I was not sure that I would remain in the U.S.

A little verse I wrote (March, 1906) reveals what my psychology was prior to emigrating to the United States. It also reflects the European idea of that day that the United States was the place to make money, but by implication, not necessarily the best place to live. This verse I had forgotten, but came across it after it had lain hidden for 60 years in a diary I had kept at the time.

On Going to America
March 1906

"Querist,[1] hearken unto this
Stewart Scrimshaw, not amiss

---

[1] An inquirer - Ed.

Says "Abroad I'm going soon
Time will be at April's moon."

What! Leave England? Yes 'tis sure!
Hard may't be, but joyous more
Greater will my powers be
When life afresh shall come to me.
Ask you where I go, and rates?
Heark, I say, United States
There to live and work for gold
England live when wealth to hold.
Ohio state is, dear friend,
My place for a time to spend
When have I knowledge gained, shall move
And shall then any wisdom prove.
Opportunities I'll grasp.
Then you'll see I'll not be last.
Being young and fresh to learn,
I will merit what I earn
Some may ask, "Where do you list?"
Ah! My friend, that must be whist.[2]
Tell you then will I, when time
Brings sweet life in me its prime.
Wise you're not, say some, to go
Live in lands you do not know.
What of that! It matters not.
Mine is not another's lot.
Some think they their own have made
When 'twas done by others' aid.
'Help yourself,' said Smiles, and find
That you will not be left behind
A selfish life is not my aim
For such I would refrain.
But, say I, thine own uphold
To bring thee joy and that untold.

---

[2] That must be kept silent

Time creeps on, and soon I'll greet
Coronia, on which I'll meet
Ocean waves in western seas
Where I hope to ride with ease.

Now that England I must leave
Wish I do that none would grieve
If permitted should I be
To return when twenty-three,
All will say 'Twere happy day
That bore thee so far away.
Land of birth so fair and free
Thought of thee doth make me glee.'
Parents, brothers, sisters all,
Friends so dear I would recall.
Hard it is to leave you here
But I must not grieve or fear.
Now at last I make the move.
Onward 'til the end I prove
Goodbye, England, old and true
Welcome now to England New.
Friends so fair and kind and true
At last Farewell! To all of you.

On April 8, 1906, after farewells in my hometown of Boston, there were assembled at my brother's home in Spalding, my mother, and two sisters and a few other friends to give me a good "send-off." This was Sunday and it was made a festive day with evening filled with singing of hymns, a phenomenon quite customary in those days. Incidentally, I have been humming some of the tunes subconsciously from that day to this.

Monday morning, April 9, 1906 at 10:15 I entrained for Liverpool as I listened to my family and friends bid me "Bon Voyage." I arrived in Liverpool that night and stayed at what was then 31-33 Union Street for 4 shillings (at that time almost the equivalent of an American dollar). The next day, April 10, about 12 noon, I went to the landing stage and embarked on the Cunard Steam Ship *Coronia* lying in the harbor (this ship was torpedoed in World War I. The latter day *Coronia* is a replacement.)

On the next day 500 passengers embarked at Queenstown (now Cobb) all bound for the United States. This epitomized the grand rush for the New World due largely to the advertising of the shipping magnates.

The third day out we encountered a choppy sea which gave me my only experience with sea sickness. The fourth day was more the same; sea very rough. I was in bed most of the day, but managed at night to get out on the deck to listen to groups of Welshmen singing. The world knows that they do it well. The fifth day of the crossing was still very rough. This was also true of the sixth day out.

April 16, the seventh day, the sea still rough, but I was feeling better. I had to pass the doctor for examination. I was overcome by the closeness of the quarters and the resulting odors. After being taken on deck, I was eventually revived.

April 17, the deck was shut down again. I had to spend time below deck, but was not seasick.

April 18 brought the event we were waiting for. It was the sight of New York Harbor. The Statue of Liberty was pointed out to us, but its significance was to become more manifest with subsequent experience. The weather and sea were splendid. We came in the New York Harbor in the afternoon and docked about 4:30 p.m. Cabin passengers got off before those of us who were traveling third class. Because of the jam on Ellis Island with immigrants arriving at the rate of 12,000 per day, I spent two dreary days aboard ship waiting to be taken to Ellis Island.

This came to pass on April 21. We got off the ship at 8:00 a.m. and landed on Ellis Island at 12 noon. The screening process was routine. I was taken off the island about midnight and ferried to the Jersey City Pennsylvania Railroad Station. There I slept in the waiting room until morning when at 8:00 a.m. I boarded the train for Pittsburgh en route to Cleveland, Ohio.

It should be related at this point that as we arrived in New York Harbor, we were advised of the dreadful earthquake which had just occurred in San Francisco. The screaming headline made an impression on all the newcomers of that day which none will ever forget. At Ellis Island I paid for two telegrams which were never sent. It was easy for attendants to take money and to fail to fill their obligation. This practice must have put a lot of change in the pockets of some of the Ellis Island employees.

At the Pittsburgh Pennsylvania station I had a waiting period between trains. I left my baggage on a waiting room bench while I looked around in the station. An understanding gentleman took occasion to warn me not to leave my baggage unattended or I would lose it. I was learning fast. I was no longer in a homogeneous society, with generations of traditions of personal honesty, as England was before the World Wars, but in a new country, a melting pot of many peoples and cultures.

On April 23 I arrived in Cleveland at 5:00 a.m. I made the mistake of getting off the train at the Euclid Avenue Station instead of the Central "Depot" (a new name to me for a station). This station on 55th street was a long way from 611 Euclid Avenue, which was my destination. I started to walk, but soon discovered that fifty city blocks would be a most formidable task, especially while carrying all my earthly belongings in a large Portmanteau. At five o'clock in the morning it was not easy to get directions. In time, however, I discovered streetcars were going my direction and ultimately I finished my journey by taking advantage of one.

On arriving at my destination I was importuned to shave off my young mustache which revealed a European origin. I was now on my way to becoming Americanized. Cleveland, Ohio, of course, was a thrilling sight. It was a good place to become Americanized, a very impressive city with new high buildings and an up-to-date electric streetcar system. It was interesting to see the sights of this new country but my chief interest at the time was to determine when I could get to work.

Chapter II

GOING TO COLLEGE IN THE NEW WORLD

"Learning makes a man fit company for himself." - Young

In due time, after visiting with my relatives in Cleveland, and becoming more or less oriented, I made plans to get work at my trade. I therefore made appropriate inquiries. I discovered it would be necessary in Cleveland for me to become a member of the union. Consequently, I promptly made application to join the Cleveland Local Union No. 5 of the Bricklayers, Masons and Plasterers International Union. The business agent, known then by the term "Walking Delegate" of the union, secured a job for me. In due time, I was a bona-fide union craftsman and on my way to earn money for college.

Fifty-five cents per hour was the union scale. With a 44-hour week, the earnings proved to be good. Not all crafts had Saturday afternoon off. It was impressed upon me that this concession to the union of Saturday half-holiday had been won only at considerable struggle and sacrifice on the part of the union men.

At this particular time many trained and skilled workmen would be included in the stream of immigration, but there would also be those who would try to get into the union who were not qualified but who could "steal the trade" once they were admitted into the union. It might be quite possible, and sometimes it happened, that a "faker" would expect by trial and error to shortcut or abbreviate an apprenticeship. This could happen if the faker was able to work beside really skilled men for a time. When the skilled labor market was tight, he could get a job and could work for a while before he was discovered as incompetent and be fired. This could happen several times until the man learned enough to "hold his job." At the beginning of the century a man did not have a property right in his job. If he were discharged that was the privilege of the employer. The union did not protect the job of the member as an individual but only his competition.

There were two ways for a bricklayer to qualify for membership in the union. One was, obviously, the right to full membership after a bona-fide apprenticeship. The other was through getting fellow craftsman to sign a voucher to the effect that he had observed the work of the potential member and could certify that his skill justified his being admitted into the union. These vouchers, a minimum of two, were presented at the next union meeting at which time the applicant would be either accepted or rejected. Let it be said that under such circumstances the union would rarely fail to admit a candidate who was "vouched for," since if a person was able to perform the work of the craft at all, it were better for the objectives of the union that he should be accepted in the membership rather than be left out of it for unfair competition. The unions operated on the "union shop" basis which at that time was called the "closed shop."

In my case, as related above, I had served a five-year apprenticeship to learn bricklaying and plastering and had the credentials to prove it. In an old country, as one would expect, where there was relatively little new construction, much building construction work involved repairs and alterations involving at times many trades. As a consequence, while serving this apprenticeship I learned many skills in addition to the ones named, such as mosaic and other tile setting, laying sanitary drain pipes, plumbing, etc. My apprenticeship years were from 14 to 19. This was not an accident. It was a deliberate design. As intimated above, I reasoned, on my own that if I would learn a good paying trade I would ultimately finance secondary and higher education. I had chosen to learn the trade of a bricklayer because it paid well for the summer and I could go to school on the earnings in the winter.

During the time of the apprenticeship, I attended a public night school three nights per week to learn Art and Building Construction and Drawing, which proved to be a bonus for me in later years even though I gave up an earlier idea of becoming an architect or building contractor.

In another connection I have recounted how unsatisfactory, at the turn of the century, it was for a person to "work his way" through an English University. Going to college in the New World was something quite different from what it would have been in the Old where only members of the families of privilege and wealth ordinarily would be given the opportunity to go to the University. At the beginning of the century, some scholarships were established which in special cases would technically give a non-privileged person an opportunity to get to the University. However, so far as I could determine the social stratification of a class society made college uninviting to those who were not blessed with inherited privilege or wealth.[3]

The Christmas season 1906 in Cleveland, Ohio, had arrived. I had been in the country seven months by that time. I was attracted to this city in the first place because two of my father's brothers had settled on the outside of Cleveland soon after the Civil War, raised their families, and had prospered. Their land

---

[3] Subsequent to the World Wars other colleges and universities in Britain have been established providing more modern curricula designed to meet the needs of an industrial society rather than to perpetuate the class distinction which characterized the landed aristocracy.

was subsequently swallowed up by the westward expansion of the city.

Work outdoors at this time of the year was all but impossible. This, then, was the time to start pursuing my academic objectives. I had earned enough money to see me through for some time ahead. Now the question was where should I go to college. I myself knew nothing of particular schools of higher learning in the United States. One family of those mentioned above suggested I go to Western Reserve in Cleveland, and the other that I attend Oberlin. Either institution would be near enough for me to have the benefit of the advice and other felicitous manifestations of family connections. However, I elected to go further away where I could continue to make my own decisions and stand on my own feet, so to speak. This aspect of personal independence was not without its advantages. Many students said that they envied the opportunity I had to direct my own affairs. It struck me at the time that the average American college student is not put on his own as is his European counterpart. In fact, the whole educational experience for the European students takes on a more serious aspect and at an earlier age than that of the American student.

Since I was brought up as a Wesleyan Methodist, it was not surprising that a Methodist minister of a church on the west side of Cleveland, Ohio interested me in his Alma Mater, Ohio Wesleyan University. Furthermore at the time, I was prone to the idea that I myself would study for the Ministry.

It should be recalled at this point that the United States was not yet fully matured as an industrial nation. We had not yet become an urbanized society. Secondary education was not universal. It was not practical for boys and girls on the farms to have high school opportunities. Transportation was by the horse and buggy. In the rural areas it was the "little red schoolhouse" that constituted the popular schooling norm. Consequently, if a farm or country boy or girl aspired to enter college, he or she would lack college preparatory or secondary schooling. To overcome this handicap, our educational forebears responsible for the establishment of private colleges in many cases established "Academies" so that young men and women without a high school education could take college preparatory work in the Academy associated with the college. So it was for me who had spent the normal high school years learning a trade.

After World War I, with the expansion of compulsory schooling and the improvement of transportation, college academies became unnecessary and therefore soon disappeared.

On January 7, 1907, I matriculated as a "Prep" in the Ohio Wesleyan Academy in the small town of Delaware, Ohio just north of Columbus. It might be of interest to point out a few highlights of the undergraduate years. So far as "prep" work was concerned, I took qualifying examinations in English literature, Greek history, etc. I received credit for some of the evening schoolwork in Art and in Building Construction undertaken during my apprenticeship in my home town of Boston, England. The upshot of my serious thirst for knowledge resulted in spanning the three-year college preparatory work plus the full four-year undergraduate classical BA curriculum, a seven-year program, in four and two-thirds academic years.

It should be mentioned that I registered as an "adult special." I worked my way through college, aided by the borrowing of funds. There was hardly any time for play, or for what in those days was called "fussing"-- that is, cultivating the society of co-eds.

For the record, I was graduated Cum Laude June 12, 1912 with the degree of Bachelor of Arts which required the standard classical studies of that day. When I entered O.W.U. it must be born in mind that I was considered a "foreigner."

Being more mature in age and experience than the average student, many of the undergraduate boy "capers" seemed nonsensical and childish to me, and the "class rush" I thought positively barbaric. Hazing struck me as something unbecoming for young intellectuals. Naturally I was unable to fully appreciate the value of the Greek letter social fraternities and particularly their initiation activities. I was not yet Americanized.

My English accent was pronounced as evidenced by the fact that my Cleveland cousins chided me concerning it. It was my intention to become an American citizen as soon as possible. In this I was aided and abetted by the Union to which I have referred. The union required all applicants of foreign origin to take out their first naturalization papers and produce the evidence to the union before being accepted. Since I was to become an American citizen I consciously allowed, so far as I knew, to have my native accent disappear. In due time, my national origin was no longer obvious. However, this was not until after my college days.

The second and third terms of the three quarter system in 1907 were financed by the earnings of the previous summer. This was auspicious because it gave me a better opportunity to become adjusted.

During the year of 1907, there occurred a financial panic the like of which I was to learn had been of frequent occurrence in American economic history. During this period many transactions had to be made with New York Clearing House certificates. It appears that our currency was insufficiently elastic to meet the ordinary demands of commerce and at the same time to prove adequate for the demands of agriculture at the time of moving the production crops to the West. It was such experiences as this which led to the demand for reform of the currency, ultimately resulting in the passage of the Federal Reserve Act of 1913.

This situation had two aspects which have a bearing on this narrative. First, let it be said that such financial instability results in injustice and disaster for many people who could not be insulated against such a contingency. People in debt could lose their property, banks would have to close, and workers lose their jobs.

This particular financial panic was also a disaster for me, since I who needed an opportunity to earn money for the succeeding school year faced the prospect of joblessness. Building construction would be considerably curtailed and the prospect of steady summer work would be practically nil.

As a somewhat naive college student, I listened to the siren song concerning the possibility of making good money in the summer time by house-to-house canvassing to sell "Chautauqua Desks." In those days "Chautauqua" was a charmed word. The desk by that name was a child's desk with the customary blackboard and copy scrolls, etc. The way this product was presented to the prospective student salesman was to assure him that such a device was a great boon to the rising generation. The education of one's children, next to feeding them, was presumed to be the most important consideration for the parents.

The total cost of the desk was $5.75. With the sale of every desk, the student canvasser would receive $1.75. Of course the salesman had to buy his sample, hence hundreds would be sold to canvassers in the various colleges. This in itself, of course, was quite a "racket." It was claimed that selling "Chautauqua Desks" would make more money than could be made by working at a trade.

At any rate, I fell for the deal. My assigned territory was Oshkosh, Wisconsin. The desk company required a letter of credit which I obtained from one of my uncles in Cleveland, who incidentally tried to discourage me by endeavoring to impress on me that I was going out to the West among the wild Indians. At any rate when school was out I borrowed the railway fare and with a college associate, an Ohio farmer's son, entrained for Oshkosh, Wisconsin.

We followed the instructions in trying to get oriented in the community to begin our selling campaign. We engaged a room although we had no money to pay down. We expected to get this out of our earnings. Therefore, because we appeared to be honest students (which of course we were), we were extended credit. Incidentally, the credence that one person would put on another, even a stranger, was greater in that generation than it is today.

After a week's preparation we started the house-to-house canvass in separate directions. It did not take long for me to be fully disillusioned. About the third house that I canvassed, the mother with her three children around her confessed being interested in the desk, but stressed the fact that she couldn't afford the investment. She pointed out the conditions of the children's shoes, and said, "I think I should buy the children new shoes before buying the desk." I took a second look, and in violation of pre-sales instructions felt compelled to agree with her, so I said, "I think so, too, lady." I could not get myself to pressure a woman to buy the desk which one might say was, in a sense, a luxury when there was such a crying need to provide a necessity.

It should be remembered that this was a period of low wages, in a low wage town. I was told, and this seems incredible today, that in some streets where working people lived, some families sat in their homes in the dark to save the cost of kerosene for their lamps. At that time Oshkosh was the last place imaginable for a person to make any money selling a luxury item by house-to-house canvassing. I discovered a few years later that the Industrial Commission of Wisconsin had had its problems here with the enforcement of the child labor laws—a sign of the times. Remember, this was before World War I. Later I came to know the city under better conditions and came to like it very much.

Two weeks had gone by and neither one of us had sold a desk. In the meantime, I had pawned my watch for a meal ticket. My friend wrote home for money to return. For me that was impossible. My home was 4,000 miles away, across the ocean. The uncle who had loaned me the money to come west had taken a trip that summer to England. I was completely and inexorably on my own. Naturally I could not forget that I had a trade, and that if I could only find a job where I could work, I could come through. I started to scour the town to find an opportunity for a job at my trade. I discovered that there was only one building being constructed in the city and that was a building being put up by the Diamond Match Company. I decided to try and get a job on this building.

I approached the builder and told him that I was a brick-layer and was looking for a job. He looked at me and I am sure he thought I was an imposter. He said he couldn't use any more bricklayers. I asked him if he would mind if I took a look around the job. To this he consented. On inspecting the building I discovered that on one wall there was a place for another man, which would definitely even up the spacing per man, to make the production more efficient. I then returned to the builder and told him that there was a place for another man on the south wall. After being in school nine months, I certainly did not appear to be a construction mechanic. There were no indications to suggest that I might be an outdoor worker. He looked at me rather quizzically and said, "I really believe that you are a brick-layer, after all, but you're the 'damnest whitest' bricklayer I've ever seen. Come around and see me in a couple of weeks."

"Two weeks," I said. "That's impossible. I'd starve to death in the meantime. I need a job now!"

"All right," he said, "come around in the morning." I told him I would, but that I had no tools with me. He said that he would loan me the necessary tools to start.

Now the die was cast. I had no money. I borrowed 50¢ from the Y.M.C.A. Secretary. This was possible because I was a bona-fide college student. Twenty-five cents of this I paid for a pair of rather thin white Oshkosh overalls, and fifteen cents for a "Wool-worth" straw hat. Ten cents remained for one day's streetcar fare to take me there and back.

The next morning I went to work. When I put on my over-alls, with the fifteen-cent hat, I must have looked like a scarecrow.

The workmen sitting around certainly must have thought I was a fake, although they were "game." However, since the bricklayers that morning had to wait until the carpenters built a scaffold, there was much conversation among them for my benefit. They were trying to scare me by saying how much harder they worked in Oshkosh than they did in Chicago, intimating that it would be unlikely that I could "hold a job."

Finally I took my place on the scaffold to work on the wall. I was on a stretch between two window openings where two of us, one on one end and one on the other, would work towards the center. Each of us was to lay half of the length. My partner started out to "show me up." He worked three parts of the length and I one part on the first course. Since I was "getting my hand in," I permitted this with the plan of adding an extra brick or two length with each successive course. In a relatively short time, I was doing more than my part of the wall's length.

Two or three hours later the builder came to me and said, "I knew you were a mechanic as soon as you picked up the trowel. I want you to go over to another part of the building and establish a corner." Now I was "in." However, the day was hot – 102° in the shade. By three o'clock in the afternoon I was overcome with the heat, and was very sick, and had to quit work and lie down in the shade, beside the building wall. The men on the job were sure that I was finished and would not be back the next day. Later when I had partially recovered, somebody took me to a house across the street for a cup of tea. It helped me to revive, after which I took the street car to my rooming house and went to bed.

The next morning I was up and back to the job on time. The workmen on the job were wonderful. They "opened up" and appointed one of their number to go down the line and collect a dollar from each person to loan to me until payday. Not even my professional associates could do any better than that. Of course, I told them I was a union man, and that I had sent for my "traveling card." They took me on faith. It was a heart-warming experience.

A few weeks later a man came around to recruit bricklayers for the building of a new Post Office in Escanaba, Michigan. Thinking of my return to Cleveland at summer's end on a Great Lakes steamer, I thought it would be good to accept. So I promised I would go to Escanaba. I gave notice to the Oshkosh builder and in due time, one evening I went to his office to collect my pay. He tried to persuade me to stay with him for the rest of the summer, promising to raise my wages and give me the "best work available."[4]

I was sorry I had promised the other man, but having inherited or acquired the idea that a person should honor his word, I felt I must go through with it. So I went to Escanaba, Michigan to work on a new Post Office building of classic design (this building has long since been superceded by another).

While in Escanaba I made a few friends. I became acquainted with the minister of a local church. This man was great in his calling, but didn't know how to handle his financial affairs. He borrowed $25 from me, which was a fortune for a student in 1907. I was an easy mark. Three years later I received $2.50 on account. The remainder I finally had to write off. It certainly hurt not to have had that $25 when I returned to school that September. However, I learned a lesson I never forgot, as the reader can well imagine.

Another significant connection I made in Escanaba was the family of the superintendent of the city schools. There were in this town at the time only three automobiles. One was owned by the local building contractor, one by the playboy son of a well known Wisconsin lumber baron, and the third by the superintendent of schools whose car was named by the townspeople "The Pinafore." I was told that the high school had presented

---

[4] Meaning work demanding the highest skill.

for public entertainment the comic opera HMS Pinafore. It had been a marked success, and the people said that the proceeds from this opera were used to buy the auto for the superintendent. Whatever may have been the facts, I myself did not take the story too seriously. I became acquainted with the family and found his charming daughter to be good company.

I was invited one Sunday to take an outing with the family in the automobile. An automobile journey in 1907 was quite a thrill. We rode to Gladstone, Michigan, and took the car on a ferry boat to Washington Island. This automobile was the first auto on this island. We drove all around the island and took note of the severe looking houses, for the most part painted white which I was told were built and settled by Icelanders. This was the one and only time I saw Washington Island which I learned has since become a coveted place in the summer for many people.

I did not return by the Great Lakes. It would have taken too much time. When you earn by the hour, time is money.[5]

After the one summer's unfortunate experience with house-to-house canvassing to earn college expenses, I subsequently worked at my trade to obtain finances. I managed to convince the business manager of the University of my competency to

---

[5] There is a sequel to the above story which seems to confirm that "Truth really is stranger than fiction." Ten years after this date, I had become, as related elsewhere, the State Supervisor of Apprenticeship for Wisconsin. A meeting was called of Building Contractors on the subject of apprentices. The Oshkosh builder who had employed me ten years earlier was among the group. When he arrived, I asked him if he remembered putting up the building in Oshkosh for the Diamond Match Co. in 1907, and did he remember hiring a college student who was the "damnest, whitest bricklayer he had ever seen?" He looked at me with amazement. He could hardly believe it. I suppose that it was hard to think a person whom he had known as a bricklayer could be an officer of the State Industrial Commission. Now, I was a state official with some degree of administrative power. Before me was a "client" so to speak, who ten years earlier had been my employer and had given me a lift when I was practically "down and out." One never knows what the vicissitudes of life may bring.

make repairs on University buildings. I took specific jobs on a verbal contract basis and worked between classes on free days. Sometimes I hired a fellow student to help. The first job I undertook was to point up the joints of Merrick Hall, a limestone structure three stories high. I acquired a second hand painter's swinging scaffold and kept it hanging for any intermittent use. Another job was to replace the eroded limestone window sills on Sturges Hall, another three-story building. I made new sills of concrete to replace the old. This kind of use of leisure hours prevented any participation in college sports, except for performance as a gymnast.

By the time I was halfway through college, my trade skill became known in the community. Hereby hangs a tale. A mason by the name of Sherman was installing a tiled fireplace unit in a new house for the owner of the town lumber company. Before the job was half finished, he died. Since he was a fellow member of the local union, I volunteered to finish the job so that the widow could receive pay for it. The execution of this job impressed the supply house in the town that sold the fireplace equipment, tile hearths, etc. Consequently, they sold their fireplace units on the understanding that I could install them. Customers would have to wait until I could find the time. After this, most weekends would have a job waiting for me. On Friday night I could take out the old unit and on Saturday install the new. Each job paid $5.00 by agreement. Two dollars of this went for room rent and three dollars for board. In those days before World War I, this was quite an achievement.

The summer following graduation I was importuned to manage the erection of a commercial garage. This experience resulted in some of the town's businessmen trying to persuade me to set up a building construction business in town. Strangely enough, the Supply House referred to begged me to take time off from graduate work, which I began at the University of Wisconsin, to return to Delaware, Ohio to install the tiling in a new mausoleum. They may have stipulated in a contract that I would do the tiling, not knowing that I was committed to pursue graduate studies with a view toward a career with more human interest then building construction. I had to decline their flattering offer.

Since this story centers around a career steeped in sociological and economic problems impinging on human relations in industry, it is fitting to recall some of the significant stimuli of my undergraduate days.

In April, 1908, my freshman year, I attended a series of lectures identified as "Merrick Lectures" in the area of "The Social Application of Religion." These lectures must have helped to condition my social responses. A recital of the specific lectures, each of which I attended, gives an index to the temper of the times. The first lecture was by the Rev. Charles Stelzle entitled "The Spirit of Social Unrest," the second by the well-known Jane Addams of Hull House, Chicago, on the subject "Women's Conscience and Social Amelioration," the third by Dr. Graham Taylor on the subject "Industry and Religion," and the final lecture of the series by Dr. George P. Eckman on "Christianity and the Social Situation."

In the first two years of college R.O.T.C. military training was required. The aftermath of the Civil War was still apparent. After all, only 42 years had elapsed since it closed. I won the honor of the best cadet in my company and received a coveted cross guns decoration. Later I became a gymnast and was elected to the honorary gymnast fraternity of Gamma Theta.

On October 12, 1909 there was organized the Ohio Wesleyan Social Service League. In its stated purpose were the words "to create a greater interest in social service, to study social movements, to initiate social service. . . ."

The program for the weekly meetings during that Fall term was socialism. This proved to be very enlightening, and of particular interest to me. It brought to light some of the seedy side of our much vaunted industrial progress. It aroused in me a passion to help the "underdog." It is but fair to say that my appraisal of socialism itself was negative, although I found some articles written by socialists to be very stimulating. In discussions during our college debates I discovered that I could quote to great effect passages from editorials of the socialist newspaper, *Appeal to Reason,* written by Eugene V. Debs. Some of the statements seemed to surprise my fellow students at times, but the end result was a greater appreciation of the basic cause of the socialist ideology and a wider range of ideas concerning the sociological issues of the day. The brand of Socialism discussed at the time could be classified as Christian Socialism. During the following term the subject of study was "The Relation of the Church to Social Service Movements." Incidentally in my senior year I served as secretary of this organization.

This social service league was symptomatic of the first decade of this century. People with a social conscience realized that there were serious unsolved social problems that needed attention. One of the first of these to register among college students of the day was the problem of Americanization of the immigrants. During my undergraduate days Jacob Riis of New York City visited the college. His presentation of the problem of the immigrants and our responsibility to them was most pointed.

November 8, 1909 there was organized in the University a Cosmopolitan Club. This I think was the second college organization to which I became attached. I served as its president. There was a good representation of foreign students, at that time, mainly possible because of Christian Missions around the world. No Fulbright-type scholarship existed in those days. The club accentuated my interest in international affairs which has always been a subject of deep concern to me.

In my junior year there was a lecture by Professor Walter Rauschenbusch on "Christianizing the Social Order."

At this time the college had about a dozen literary societies devoted to parliamentary law and public speaking. There were intersociety and also interclass contests in speech and debate, in which I participated. To express oneself properly in public address was a serious objective of most of the students of that day. The establishment of public speaking instruction in the college curriculum finally caused the abolition of the literary societies, which incidentally were given Greek names such as Athenian, Clionian, Amphictyonian, and Chrastomathian. They were wonderfully effective aids for self-improvement.

Ohio Wesleyan School of Oratory, now named "School of Speech," was an influence that helped to popularize public speaking. It was to me more than that. It brought to the college a young woman to do graduate work in speech, who came to the campus in my senior year. Being president of a young people's church society which at the time gave a party to new students, it was my obligation to express to this person appreciation for her part in entertaining the group with a dramatic reading. I was impressed by her ability and personality. At the end of my college course, I thought I could afford to cultivate her acquaintance. This I did, and a few years later we were married. This proved to be the most fortunate experience of my life. As I pen these lines we have reached beyond our Golden Wedding Anniversary.

In my junior year I won the first prize in the poetry contest.

In my senior year at the Class Day Commencement Exercise, I was appointed the Class Poet.

As one sees things in retrospect, it is easy to understand how early aspirations to be a Methodist minister, with the emphasis on individual lives, were superceded by a consuming desire to have a career in the area of improving human relations in industry. I was impressed at a relative early age with the cleavage between principles of Christianity I had learned early in life and their application or rather lack of application to the conduct of most of the business and industrial enterprise, that is so far as human relations was concerned.

The year 1912 was in many ways epochal in respect to the

evolution of my personal experience with industrial relations. In that year it was my good fortune to be graduated from Ohio Wesleyan University with an undergraduate major in economics. I wrote an honors paper on the history of the Bricklayers, Masons and Plasterers International Union. At the time, I was a member of a local union in Delaware, Ohio. In February of 1912, I had attended as a delegate the national convention of the union in St. Joseph, Missouri and was initiated into the political mysteries of big unionism. I discovered a tremendous amount of idealism and integrity among the delegates, especially those representatives from relatively small local unions. It was rather disillusioning, however, to find collusion between the delegates from the largest unions to control the convention. If Chicago and New York delegates agreed to a matter, it would be almost certain to carry the convention. The delegates from the smaller unions would be numerically superior, but it would be impossible to get the organized solidarity necessary to outvote the designs of the combination of the delegates from the nation's two largest unions in the craft. This kind of phenomenon accounts for much of the unsavory aspects of big unionism.

Sometime previous to this, while a university student, I had attended the Ohio State Conference of the union, at Bellaire, Ohio. This was a relatively new organization. I found myself being nominated as a candidate for the office of President of the Ohio Conference. I am sure I must have given the impression to the "old timers" of an "upstart." One outstanding Scotch Irishman, a very intelligent man, was running in opposition. He was an experienced person in union matters and not unaccustomed to political techniques. I was soundly defeated, although the defeat was an honorable one because I did not seek the office. It was a lesson.

However, the man who won the office—who was old enough to be my father—came to me afterwards and said he didn't like the manner of the election campaign and consequently thought he would teach me, or those who were backing me, a lesson. He expressed the wish to have me maintain my interest and come up for office at a later time. The man indicated that had I talked to him before the election he might have retired in my favor. He exhibited a very fine spirit and was really interested in my developing maturity in union politics. This was experience for me. However, I was not, in any sense, seriously committed to a career as a labor leader. My interest in the union and its functioning was purely sociological.

1912 was a national election year, and a very interesting election it was. Woodrow Wilson was opposed by William Howard Taft, and also by a Third Party, known as the "Bull Moose Party," headed by Theodore Roosevelt. The country was in ferment. Reform was in the air. The Socialist Party under the leadership of Eugene V. Debs polled approximately one million votes. This fact in many respects seemed to shock the country. It was apparent that free immigration had given an opportunity to American employers for the exploitation of the labor market to their own advantage. This resulted in significant social unrest.

Another aspect of free immigration was the importation of European ideologies, including Anarchism, Marxism, Fourierism, Owenism, Syndicalism, etc. These helped to create among the industrial workers a confusion of ideas, which generated many clashes, not only between workers and employers but between organizations of workers and ethnic groups. It can easily be appreciated that since there was a steady supply of potential employees arriving daily at Ellis Island, New York, it was very difficult for many labor organizations to thrive. Language barriers also complicated matters. In the skilled occupations craft unions were possible, but in the political and social environment of the time, organization for collective bargaining was practically impossible in the mass production industries.

The labor injunction was a strong defense weapon of the employer. The matter of restricting the use of injunctions in labor disputes was a campaign issue of the Bull Moose Party. However, since there was the three-corner fight it resulted in the election of Woodrow Wilson. Wilson, a former professor and president of Princeton, was a political reformer. His election really called for a "new deal." Reform also was overdue in the American banking system. The conditions of labor were crying for public attention and for protective legislation. Organized labor was demanding the restriction of immigration as well as opposing injunctions.

By the time I was a senior in college I had determined to pursue graduate study in the field of economics, particularly in labor economics. The question was where? Two universities were leaders in the field of labor economics at that time, namely Wisconsin and Columbia. The decision of where to go was not too difficult to determine since there were factors which conditioned my decision in favor of Wisconsin. For example, although my economics professor had received his doctorate from Columbia he nevertheless adopted the Wisconsin economic textbook by Richard T. Ely. Furthermore the textbook studied in the course of labor problems, or labor economics, was written by T. S. Adams and Helen Summer, both of the University of Wisconsin.

Adams and Summer's textbook on labor problems was a standard text for many years. Its first copyright was in 1905. Its latest edition as far as I can determine was 1922. Incidentally, the particular subject matter of this early text tells eloquently what were the outstanding problems of the day. A comparison of this pre-World War I textbook with the textbook of the '60's would show how far we have traveled since the beginning of the century. The Adams and Summer text contained thirteen chapters. The leading subjects presented were Woman and Child Labor, Immigration, and the Sweating System (Sweat Shop Operations). There was also a chapter on Profit Sharing exemplified by the plan of Proctor & Gamble Company. It is well to note that this company still prospers in the sixties, which speaks well for the foresight and humanity of its founders. One chapter was devoted to the Agencies of Industrial Peace, namely, Conciliation and Arbitration, Compulsory Arbitration, and Collective Bargaining. Another chapter examined the question of Industrial Education, a subject destined to receive future public attention and social action. A system of industrial education did not exist at the time although there was a crying need.

From the above it was apparent that an interesting field of study was in the offing. Subsequent experience was to determine that distinguished careers were to be built on the effort to solve these major problems, and significant improvements in our industrial society were to be wrought as a consequence. I was conditioned by this time for further study, and how this materialized is explained in the following chapter.

Chapter III

GRADUATE SCHOOL - FOUNDATIONS OF A CAREER

The more extensive a man's knowledge of what has been done, the greater will be his power of knowing what to do.
Benjamin Disraeli

In September 1912 I enrolled as a graduate student in economics at the University of Wisconsin. In Wisconsin we were getting the impact of the successful Progressive Party under the leadership of Senator Robert M. La Follette. The University of Wisconsin at this time was keenly interested in state and national affairs under the wise guidance of its farsighted president, Charles Van Hise.

Initiation into a graduate school was an experience to remember. I landed in Madison in September a few days before the beginning of school. After getting off the train at the Northwestern Depot, it was necessary, because of a heavy rain, to wade through about a foot of water to get on the streetcar. However, full of expectancy I made my way to the University and then found that Richard T. Ely, the chairman of the economics department with whom I had corresponded, was in Australia. The other major professor for me to see, John R. Commons, was out of the city, engaged in some public service function.

Unfortunately, because my counselor was not available, I received poor direction and orientation for my courses. This is a more serious handicap than is realized by many university professors. Learning the hard way was and is often something which consumes too much time. The mention of this experience is to remind the reader that the more celebrated the professors are, the more interested they become in public affairs, the less accessible they are likely to be to individual students unless those individual students promise to enhance the professor in his work or to add something to his field of study. This may sound cynical but I am certain that some professors' exploitation of graduate students can, and has in many instances, been morally reprehensible. I am not referring here to any one specific experience at Wisconsin, but speaking as one sophisticated concerning the trials and tribulations of many graduate students. Of course, this exploitation can be rationalized up to a certain point on the score that the graduate student is learning a great deal, but it may result in sacrifices of time and energy on the part of the student for which he may have nothing to show. At the University of Wisconsin one of the outstanding reasons that John R. Commons achieved such renown among his students was the fact that he was generous in giving credit to the students for whatever the student accomplished. He tended to impress upon the student that his or her efforts were of more importance than that of his own. That made him a rather exceptional teacher.

Another thing to which the graduate student is subjected to in many situations and in many schools, is the circumstance of being obliged to be reconciled to two different professors, or two different departments with conflicting philosophies, or where frequently there is professional jealousy, which is by no means an infrequent disease in academic circles. This is especially hard for the student of different individual professors, when he must meet the approval of opposing factions. These situations are often tragic, and have, in certain instances, ruined potential and promising careers. The student had better find out early where his main responsibility lies. If he is caught between opposing factions, he might be well advised to try and find another institution where there might be less jeopardy in this respect.

Coming back to the matter of entering the graduate school at the University of Wisconsin, I might say that I came on a "shoe string." It was incumbent on me, therefore, to find a job to pay my way until an opportunity for a fellowship or assistantship should open up. The assistantships and fellowships were ordinarily given to the students who had been undergraduates at the University or who were already on the ground.

The first job obtained through the University students' employment office was that of a "bell boy," in the Avenue Hotel. This would furnish my board. The job lasted for about a week. I remember how repugnant to me was the idea of taking tips. It seemed to me to emphasize a condition of inferiority. This experience, as I've already said, didn't last long, for the manager of the hotel gave me orders to get the night desk man out of bed so that he could be ready to take over his night-time job. I went to the man's room twice and received his response. However, the manager had given me orders to enter his room and pull him out of bed. This I could not do. It was to me an invasion of privacy that my upbringing would not allow me to countenance. Since I was not disposed to go into the man's bedroom and pull him out of bed I was, therefore, accused of not obeying orders and consequently I was fired.

However, within a week or two I got a break. An assistant professor by the name of Gruehl of the economic staff had accepted a responsible assignment with the Milwaukee Electric Railway and Light Company. This created for me an opportunity to become an Assistant in Transportation which involved working with Professor Ralph Hess in two courses, one in Public Utilities, and the other in Principles of Railroad Transportation, both of which were important subjects at that time. This study was tied up with the then current big public issues of rate making. It was at this time that Senator Robert M. La Follette had attracted national interest in the problem of valuation of the railroads as a basis for sound rate-making.

Senator La Follette had risen in politics as a consequence of his fight against the abuses resulting from railroad monopolies. The railroads and other public utilities were establishing rates on the principle of "what the traffic will bear." The fight over public utilities was going on in other places besides Wisconsin. Tom Johnson, mayor of Cleveland, had had a hard fight against the Consolidated Street Railways of that city. A similar fight took place in Toledo, Ohio under Major Brand Whitlock to demonstrate that the public utilities did not own their rights of way, that their franchises did not exist in perpetuity, but were privileges granted to these corporations subject to the public interest. A part of the contest between these utilities and public authority was to establish a fair valuation as a basis for reasonable rates. This public question inspired courses of study in the University Department of Economics on the subject of "Value and Valuation." Rates were not to be based upon fictitious capitalization of company assets resulting from "watered stock," but upon the "physical valuation" of the properties of the corporation. Then again, some would want to fix rates according to the "value of the service." Others would claim that "cost of service" was the proper basis.

These were big issues of the first two decades of the century, which, incidentally, posed some difficult problems for our legislatures, administrative bodies, and the courts. Wisconsin's Senator La Follette succeeded in promoting an Act of Congress to provide for the physical valuation of the railroads. A controversial issue arose as to whether "good will" should be capitalized and included to provide a proper basis for rate-making purposes.

Teaching in the field of Transportation and Public Utilities, therefore, at this time was an engaging enterprise, particularly the opportunity to learn of the operation of regulative bodies such as the Wisconsin Railway Commission and the Interstate Commerce Commission.

However, although this experience as Assistant in Transportation was a great help to me in connecting with the University of Wisconsin's economics faculty, the subject matter at that time did not appeal to me as having sufficient human interest for a career. It was a great satisfaction, therefore, to learn that at the end of the academic year, 1912-1913, I could be appointed for the following year as the graduate assistant to Professor John R. Commons. Since my prime interest was in Labor Economics, I accepted this appointment. Now my career was having an auspicious beginning.

It seems to me that nothing can be more satisfying to a person with intellectual curiosity than to be a full-time graduate student. After a good undergraduate experience, the opportunity to join the ranks of the scholars and philosophers presents a tremendous challenge. However, while it is axiomatic that the goal of an educated person is the attainment of broad interests and culture, nevertheless, it is a fact that those who gain the greatest renown are those who, in spite of a broad education, pursue a particular line of interest and who end up respectively as an authority in a specific area or in a particular study of limited dimensions. At Wisconsin in 1912 there were very noted examples of such authorities. Richard T. Ely was one. He wrote for his day, what was generally conceded to be the most popular text in economics since the work of John Stuart Mill.

During the time when I was a graduate student, Professor Ely's main interest was in land economics. He was interested in problems of land reform. The first graduate study paper that I prepared at Wisconsin—on the subject of land tenure in Ireland—was presented at the general economic seminar which took place every Thursday evening and was attended by all members of the economics faculty. There was no credit for this course. It was an opportunity for younger scholars to meet with those of mature experience. The discussions were general. It really was an opportunity for the student to try out his ideas and profit from the contributions which were the products of different minds. Moreover, it was an opportunity for the faculty to get the "measure" of the aspirants for graduate degrees in economics.

Professor T. Adams, referred to earlier, who had first written the best book on labor problems, was also an authority on taxation and a proponent of the income tax legislation which up to this time had not yet become a reality. However, it was soon destined to become so in Wisconsin by the Income Tax Law of 1911, and for the Federal government by the 16th amendment to the United States Constitution in 1915. Professor Adams was one of the chief architects of both the Federal income tax law and that of the state of Wisconsin.

On the other side of the faculty aisle, so to speak, was Professor John R. Commons, who at the time was engaged in the major undertaking of writing the history of trade unionism in the United States, under a special Carnegie grant. This was a wonderful conjuncture of circumstances for students of labor economics.

Richard T. Ely was known as the expositor of economic theory, although it would be unfair not to recognize that the career of Professor Ely also dealt principally with the forces in the economic arena. Professor John R. Commons was characterized by his students and others as a practical economist, which indeed he was. However, although concerned mainly with reform in labor and management relationships, he too was developing an approach to the study of economics based upon the phenomena of transactions of "going concerns" involving principles of scarcity, efficiency, custom, futurity or expectancy, and sovereignty or law. This concept of the study or analysis of economic activity is known as institutional economics. It grew in Commons' mind from the practical functioning of contending forces in the whole realm of economic transactions. All Commons' graduates were given an opportunity to participate in some aspect of this intellectual effort. The book on institutional economics was published posthumously.

As great a scholar and teacher as was John R. Commons, he needed the writing skill of a Richard T. Ely to make this book palatable for undergraduate study. Ely's outlines of economics were clearly and eloquently written which no doubt accounted for its wide use over a long period of time. Institutional economics has not "gone over" mainly, I think, because the presentation of the ideas was expressed in too abstract terms, and not communicated in such a way as to arrest the interest of the average undergraduate.

It would be a sin of omission not to mention that there was a strong German influence on economics at Wisconsin at this time. Dr. Ely himself had obtained his Doctor of Philosophy Degree from the University of Berlin. The Germans were strong on what was known as the "historical method." German University exchange professors were frequent visitors at Wisconsin. There was a Professor Zinsheimer whose main thesis was the study of technological changes in industry. In his class I think I made the first study on technological changes in building construction in this country. Such a study today would take a regiment of scholars to determine, as the modern student can imagine.

Another German economist who made a negative impression on me was a Professor Bonn, whose mission seemed to me to be to prove the morality of Pan-Germanism, and to sell a philosophic rationale for the German Reich to take over colonial territories from other powers. In the field of literature was a Professor Kuehleman whose afternoon public lectures were definitely German propaganda. It was the day of philosopher Friedrich Nietzsche and the German "Superman."

To a person like me who was born in England, this propaganda seemed very ominous. On top of all this, as a member of the University of Wisconsin International Club it was necessary for me to listen to some of the German student members parade their arrogant feelings of superiority with the certain conviction that the "super race" was destined to be the "top of the heap." This was the eve of World War I, and when it commenced, these same people were certain they were to be the winners, because they believed that the pleasure-loving enemies were peoples who had become effeminate and therefore were weaklings.

It is a strange coincidence that the same day that a lecture was given by Professor Bonn at a luncheon meeting at the University Club, where he expounded the German doctrine of Lebensraum, there came a message that the Germans had declared war on Austria and were mobilizing for action.

The defeat of Germany in the ultimate outcome of World War I frustrated the efforts of the Pan-Germans to infiltrate the discourse at the University of Wisconsin.

Reference has already been made concerning the first year of graduate study at the University of Wisconsin when it was my fortune to be an assistant in transportation in the Department of Economics. However, the second year I was appointed assistant to Professor John R. Commons since labor economics was my real interest. At this time "John R.," as he was called by all his students, was serving as a member of the United States Commission on Industrial Relations. This resulted in my having to take over the class on labor legislation when John R. was away on hearings of the Commission. The overall academic interest in this particular year was the writing of a textbook on Principles of Labor Legislation. Of the graduate students enrolled in this class, about a half dozen or more were assigned topics that were to be included in the text. These advanced students were assigned to guide the undergraduates in writing term topics which would have some relation to the graduate student's assignment. As John R.'s assistant, I had the responsibility of supervising the undertaking. Of course, the main plan of the book, the determination of the chapter titles and the mainspring of ideas were products of the Master. My own specific assignment was to prepare a section of 12,000 words on the subject of Individual Bargaining. This involved an analysis of the law and of legislation which had a bearing on employees individual labor contract.

The system described above was undertaken in order that the book might be prepared for publication within a year's time. In the spring of 1914 when the book was nearing completion, John R. informed me that John Andrews, the executive director of the American Association for Labor Legislation, expressed the desire to become a joint author with Commons on the book. Andrews was a former student of Commons and, no doubt because he was so active in the institutional effort of promoting labor legislation, thought it was logical that he should be joint author. Although John R. had not anticipated this turn of events and had no enthusiasm for the deal, he was not a person to fight about priority or ideas, and so consented. The textbook was published, therefore, under the names of Commons and Andrews. For a number of years extending into the 1920's, this was an authoritative and popular text on labor legislation.

However, the sad thing about such a work is the fact that like so many effective enterprises, the degree of success is measured by the rapidity of its obsolescence. The education of a generation to understand and appreciate protective labor legislation was bound to bring about many changes and improvements. Today a textbook on protective labor legislation would be obsolete by the time it would be written. This I can testify from my experience in teaching university classes on the subject of labor legislation. Every time state legislatures meet, new laws are added or old statutes amended. Furthermore, since the 1930's, the Federal government has also entered this field, and it is no mean feat to keep up with the new enactments of Congress.

Following the second year of graduate study at the University of Wisconsin, I found it necessary to do something during the summertime to earn my "bread and butter," so naturally I sought and found an opportunity to work at my trade. It seems that the Gishholt Manufacturing Company on the east side of Madison was putting up a new building. Without difficulty I got a job on this construction. I lived in the so-called Latin Quarter, the area where faculty and students live. I went over town on the streetcar every morning. I changed my clothes on the job. In the afternoon after my eight hours, I changed again and returned to the Latin Quarter. Nobody was the wiser, but I was growing that much the richer.

In the following academic year I was granted a fellowship with the Industrial Commission of Wisconsin. This was an arrangement worked out between the University and the state government of Wisconsin which, at that time, was controlled by the "Progressive Republican" party. The idea was to have a person to work half time in the capital and to spend the other half on his graduate studies at the University. This was a very profitable arrangement both from the standpoint of the "fellow" and the Commission. Not only did the Industrial Commission have these fellowships, but the Railway Commission, and the Tax Commission had similar work arrangements, with the consequence that quite a number of good public servants were trained for Wisconsin State service and remained in it to build a career.

During this year with the Commission there were many other special assignments I had to do from time to time. In other words, I was somewhat of a student "economic expert" errand boy. I made certain investigations for the Commission. I was asked to go to places like Beloit and Sheboygan, where some labor trouble rumors, blacklisting, or something of that sort was reported. I had to make inquiries to find out what the real situation was. Of course, such experience was an eye opener and it was good training. In many ways these beginnings enlarged my economic and social horizons and indicated career possibilities of considerable human interest.

In 1911 the Wisconsin Legislature passed an apprenticeship law. This proved unsatisfactory and was not enforced. It was repealed by the passing of a new law in 1915. Nothing like this law had been on the books in any country before. Any prior legislation in this country on the apprenticeship question reached as far back as 1848, and then only to amend or modify the existing law which had been based on the common law practices and traditions of the craft guilds of earlier centuries. There was now the problem of a scarcity of skilled craftsmen. Furthermore, there was the fact that many employers were hiring boys under the pretense of apprenticeship, yet not really teaching the boys a trade. It was a way of getting cheap labor. In plain English it was pure exploitation. This new apprenticeship law was to avoid exploitation on the one hand and to promote efficient, effective apprenticeship training on the other. As we have related in other sections of this record, vocational education was being promoted and emphasized at that particular time. The need for industrial training was very great. Immigration was no longer supplying skilled workmen. In fact, the supply of labor was being curtailed because of the outbreak of World War I. The need for training young men for the skilled trades was keenly felt.

This apprenticeship statute required a fulltime administrator to make it effective. It promised a new and challenging experience for somebody. I, myself, thought that such an assignment was my opportunity. When the Civil Service Commission advertised the examination for this post, I naturally made every effort to succeed as well as possible in preparing myself as a candidate for this office. It can be related that at this time a career such as this promised to be, was a very rare opportunity. Consequently, a considerable number of people were anxious to have a chance to get such a position. The examination consisted of two parts. One was an essay written by the candidate on the subject of apprenticeship and the second was an interview, or rather an interrogation, held in Milwaukee before a group representing manufacturers, labor leaders, and vocational educators. This group was assembled by the Civil Service Commission.

During the summer of 1915 I was taking care of the apartment of the University of Wisconsin's psychology professor, Dr. Joseph Jastrow, while he was vacationing in the state of Maine. This apartment was very spacious and had a splendid library with an atmosphere conducive to study. Undisturbed, I prepared for the Civil Service examination for two whole weeks. With all the pertinent books I could put my hands on, I read studiously. At the end of these two weeks, I wrote my paper. Being saturated with the subject and able to tell the story without technical references and notes, I wrote what the Civil Service Commission later informed me was judged to be the number one paper. At the oral examination in Milwaukee, I remember the questions coming up about my being a graduate apprentice in a trade and that I had a union card. Most of the employers at that time were not in favor of unions. I thought that this might count against me but instead, it was apparently somewhat of an asset. The interesting thing about it is that even those anti-union employers in the manufacturing industries did not mind my union card so long as it was in a building trades union. It would be the other fellow's "ox that was being gored," so to speak.

On the other hand the building trades, as well as the printing industry, were strongly unionized. My trade union affiliation was to their liking. However, I was not the only candidate among the 175 applicants that had a union card, but I was the only one who had accumulated an apprenticeship, a university degree, and three years of graduate school in economics majoring in the field of labor. Since this position required breaking new ground and establishing a system of administration in a brand new public enterprise, it appeared to the Industrial Commission that I was a "natural" for the undertaking. At any rate, I was appointed as the state supervisor of apprenticeship at the then modest salary of $1500 per year.

I started on my duties November 1, 1915. As suggested above, there were no precedents for my work. This was to be the first public supervised apprenticeship in history. Naturally the procedure for administration could not have been previously determined. However, one thing was established by the law and that was that the powers of the Industrial Commission were to be applied for the administration of the law. The administration involved getting the confidence of employers, labor leaders and others so that they would cooperate. It should not be taken for granted that everybody was in favor of this law. As a matter of fact, there were quite a number of employers who resented the fact that the state Industrial Commission could come in and tell them how to run their apprenticeship system, or to suggest to them whether they should or should not have apprentices. However, it must be understood that the state of Wisconsin did not say to the manufacturers, through this piece of legislation, that they must have apprentices. The only compulsion was that in case they had apprentices, they must have these apprentices according to certain stipulations and conditions provided by the law. Of course, one of the main functions of the administrative authority was to promote apprenticeship, to persuade employers to take apprentices, and to get the labor unions to cooperate in the endeavor.

One of the first hurdles that had to be crossed was to obtain the cooperation of one or two individuals in Milwaukee who were publicly critical of the whole program. One man was Chris Sholke who was then the Works Manager of the Nordberg Manufacturing Company. The other union man was known as "Injunction Tom"--Tom Neacy, who frequently obtained court injunctions against attempts to curtail the businessman's exercise of his freedom. Both of these were very thoroughgoing individualists. They must have been the spiritual forerunners of the "John Birchers" of the 1960's. Both men had apprentices in their plants, but they could see no value in state interference. They didn't like innovations or radical departures from the status quo.

The International Harvester Company had a man stationed

in Milwaukee named Van Scoy. He was really a "king maker"-- a person of great influence. I was advised that he was the first man that I should interview. If I could get past Van Scoy, Chris Sholke, and Tom Neacy, then I was in. Naturally, I tackled these men first. As a sign of the times, it might be interesting to relate that I was told that I had better not dress the same way to see Van Scoy as I would to see the labor leaders. In other words there was still some remnant of the European class-consciousness in Milwaukee. Of course, this made no great impression on me. Newly arrived immigrants may have been class conscious, but not the native American worker. At any rate, I couldn't be one thing to one person and a different thing to another. I had no trouble making terms with Van Scoy. As far as the labor leaders were concerned, I had a union card. I could talk their language. I didn't need any cheap politician to tell me how to behave or what to think.

The works manager of a large manufacturing plant was another thing. I remember going to see Chris Sholke and he told me to come into his office. He spent an entire hour, using very emphatic unorthodox English, to impress upon me that nobody from the Wisconsin Industrial Commission could tell him how to conduct his apprenticeship, etc., etc. While I was listening to the tirade for the whole period, I realized I wasn't getting anywhere. So I very politely thanked the gentlemen and told him I would see him again at some later date. After a lapse of a few weeks, I went to see him a second time about this apprenticeship, and had to listen to another similar tirade for about an hour. When he finished, I thanked him and left him as before, telling him that I would come again sometime. In the meantime I talked to his subordinate, the general foreman, to see if he was interested in having apprentices under the Wisconsin Plan. The foreman said that he, himself, was, but the boss wouldn't allow it. So I asked him if in the case that his boss would consent, would he be in favor of it. He assured me that he would. This was the easy response to my question since he was thoroughly convinced that his boss would never consent.

The third time I called on the works manager, he started the same tirade as before. Suddenly he realized that he was repeating himself. He said, "I've told you all that before, haven't I? Let me take you out and show you our machine shop." Of this he was very proud.

As we walked along in what impressed me as a machine shop of huge proportions, it was evident that this establishment was well managed, orderly and clean. I told him, "This shop is unusually clean. It must be quite a problem to maintain such good shop housekeeping."

The man turned around, flabbergasted. He looked me right in the eye and said, "You are the first 'blankety blank' that ever came from the state capitol that showed an understanding of our shop problems, or seemed able to appreciate what we do. You are O.K."

After our shop survey, he invited me to lunch. Here I met some other members of the firm. Before leaving I then told him inasmuch as he excelled in many things, I expected he would have the best plan of apprenticeship training in his industry. Then came the pay-off. He said he wouldn't object to signing up apprentices, but that his general foreman would not go for it. Each had been sure the other would object. Without making it embarrassing, I lined up with the foreman a plan of operation. When the boss learned about it later, he was surprised but did not stand in the way.

The motive for telling this incident is to point out that some of the leading employers resented a law which would lay down the terms of operation of a program which individual employers thought they knew better how to perform than legislators or any state administrative official. The big job was to sell the program to the employers. Employers were ordinarily suspicious of state employees whom they mistakenly thought had no real experience or appreciation of the practical problems of the industry.

The employer referred to above was a very influential member of the Milwaukee branch of the National Metal Trades Association; and since he was strongly opposed to state regulation, other employers held out with him. Therefore, it was necessary to have his cooperation in order to get that of other employers. The reader can imagine that I approached this exponent of "laissez faire" with considerable trepidation.

A sequel to this story is that this same employer soon became a staunch supporter of the program and strongly proposed to the Milwaukee Metal Trade Association that it should furnish the Supervisor of Apprenticeship with an automobile so that he could more frequently get around to the apprentices in the shops of the association members. Of course, this was impracticable. If it were to be done in partnership with organized labor, it would have been possible. However, the Metal Trade employers were all anti-union, which was the reason for their membership in the Metal Trades Association. They would not be interested in any partnership with organized labor.

This apprenticeship experience intensified my interest in personnel problems, which became a subject of abiding interest in all subsequent years.

It has often been said that "Experience is the best teacher." However that may be, I can relate that it is a good teacher. I was soon to learn in a not very pleasant way the difference between theory and practice. Naturally this apprenticeship promotion was uphill work and it was difficult to make headway fast. It should be related here that the apprenticeship law was a by-product of legislation in the general field of what was, at the time, termed industrial education and continuation schooling. Wisconsin became the leader in the field due to the initiative and foresight of a dynamic Irishman by the name of Charles McCarthy, who headed the Wisconsin Legislative Reference Library. He was sent to Europe to make a study of what was being done in industrial education in European countries. On his return to Wisconsin, he persuaded the legislature to pass a law providing for Continuation Schools to "do something for working boys and girls where nothing has been done before." This was the beginning of Wisconsin legislation on vocational and adult education. The first Continuation School Law was passed in 1911.

Dr. Charles McCarthy was a person of great vision with extraordinary capacity for forceful persuasion in a good cause, but he was also a man of great impatience. During the first few months of the administration of the new apprenticeship law, it seemed to him that the number of apprentices was not increasing fast enough. In other words he expected a rash of apprentices with the passage of the 1915 law. That wasn't the way it worked. In early 1915 quite a pronounced criticism by Dr. McCarthy was publicly made on the progress the new supervisor was making. Naturally, I wasn't expecting anybody to believe that there could be great achievements within a few short months. Some things had to be built up on a long-term basis. However, when I realized that Dr. McCarthy was impatient with the progress and was making public complaints and approaching labor leaders and others to have them believe that probably the right man was not on the job, it became necessary for me to make a report. On my first apprenticeship report I showed precisely what advances had been made. The showing was very good. Moreover, the labor leaders were on my side. From that time on there was no particular criticism. The fact was that this man's enthusiasm for apprenticeship exceeded his knowledge of what an apprenticeship actually involved. I had served a five-year apprenticeship myself and I knew.

I was engaged in the business of administration of the state's new apprenticeship law from November 1, 1915 to April 3, 1920. This constituted the first major assignment of my career. I was now really on my way.

The circumstances which led me in 1920 to resign from the Industrial Commission and embark upon new fields of activity are related in Chapter VIII as one of the highlights of my career.

Chapter IV

THE "CLASSIC" ERA OF PROTECTIVE
LABOR LEGISLATION

"Industry was made for man, and not man for industry."

The generations active during the first half of this century have witnessed, if not shared in, the phenomenal growth of Protective Labor Legislation. Students during this period were unable to avoid the all-pervading atmosphere of social reform. At first they were obliged to study European antecedents. In many avenues of political and social reform the Old World was first to point the way.

Organized society has an inherent responsibility to protect its citizens. Sometimes this protection is slow in coming but eventually it arrives. Since the need for the protection of labor first became manifest in England where the industrial revolution began, we look there for American antecedents. What was termed the British "New Deal" came into being after the unpopular Boer War in South Africa (1899-1902). As first mentioned in Chapter I, the 1906 English General Election ousted the Conservative Government which had been responsible for the Boer War. People were looking for a long overdue change. There was some of the same sort of fervor for reform that later characterized the U.S. election of 1932. The Liberal Party had won the election. In the cabinet, subsequently formed, was a Labor Representative named John Burns. He was appointed head of the Board of Trade, which in many respects corresponds to our U.S. Department of Labor. He was the first labor man to become a member of the cabinet. At that time, the United States had only a "Bureau of Labor" which was not directly represented in the cabinet.

This appointment of a labor member of parliament to a cabinet post was indeed a sign of the times. This administration passed in 1906 a Workman's Compensation Law. This type of statute was designed to eliminate the injustice to workers due to the application of the Common Law which necessitated the injured person to sue for damages in the courts. It was necessary to prove that the employer (or master) was responsible before the injured worker could obtain compensation. This was usually next to impossible. It was very difficult for an injured worker to obtain compensation for injury or death. Under the common law, the employer, or master, could plead, and take refuge in any one or all of three defenses, namely: Assumption of Risk, Negligence of Fellow Servant and Contributory Negligence.

The Workman's Compensation Law abolished these common defenses of the employer, and provided for some specific compensation for loss of earnings, as well as medical care, due to accidents in the course of employment. It became not a question of who is responsible for the accident, but rather what is the extent of the injury? Formulas were set up in the statute to give employers and the administrative personnel the means to determine "compensation" due to the injured employee.

Otto von Bismarck's Germany had pioneered in the area of insurance for workers. However, in the emerging industrial society, it was Great Britain's Workman's Compensation Law that set the tone of the twentieth century era of protective labor legislation, long overdue.

In the spring of 1961, I attended a national symposium in Madison, Wisconsin to celebrate the fiftieth anniversary of the enactment of the first U. S. Workman's Compensation Act in 1911.[6]

During the summer of 1961, the U. S. Post Office Department issued a commemorative stamp to highlight the auspicious passage of that historical piece of protective labor legislation. New York had passed a Workman's Compensation Statute earlier which, because it was compulsory, was declared invalid by the Supreme Court. The Wisconsin law provided a choice for the employer. He could elect to come under the act, or elect not to come under the act. This overcame the constitutional objections of the Supreme Court. However, as time went on, for all practical purposes, the law became compulsory in all the states of the union.

Great Britain also antedated the United States in enacting the old age pension law in 1908. It made a profound impression. We in this country were beginning to feel an uneasy social conscience concerning the plight of people who reached the age when they could not, or business enterprises did not, provide them the opportunity to earn income to purchase the necessities of life and thus to avoid the necessity of having to be taken care of in the county old people's home, commonly known as the "poor house."

The Wisconsin Legislature in Chapter 185, Laws of Wisconsin, 1913, directed the Industrial Commission to make an "investigation of the number, conditions and welfare of the aged and infirm in this state with a view of establishing a system of old age pensions," and to report its findings and recommendations to the next session of the legislature.

It was my privilege and responsibility as an Industrial Commission "Fellow"[7] to be charged with the task of conducting this

---

[6] The initial administration machinery for the enforcement of this law was set up at the time the author was working for the Wisconsin Industrial Commission as a "Working Fellow" while pursuing graduate studies at the University of Wisconsin

[7] A fellowship involving half-time with the Industrial Commission and half-time as a graduate student at the University of Wisconsin.

investigation and preparing the report for the Industrial Commission.[8] This study also covered the system of old age relief in foreign countries. That report states that the "non-contributory plan of old age pensions has been adopted by Great Britain, Australia, New Zealand and Denmark." This form of relief was justified by the principle that whoever has honorably served his working life in the ranks of industry has thereby earned an honorable support in the years of superannuation. Accordingly all these laws set up more or less strict "character tests to demark the 'deserving' from the 'non-deserving' aged poor." At the same time the relief is confined by means of property and income limits, to persons in actual need.

This report was submitted to the Wisconsin Legislature of 1915. However, it received little attention, no doubt partly because it was the time of World War I. As far as I am able to recollect, the only institution to take advantage of this report was the Eagles Club which did effective lobbying to promote state old age pensions prior to the establishment of the Federal Social Security system. The official copy of the report referred to was limited and soon out of print and unobtainable. The officers of the Eagles Club borrowed the typewritten manuscript from my personal file.

The British Old Age Pension Act, passed in 1908 and revised in 1911, was the outcome of 25 years agitation during which five parliamentary commissions had investigated the subject and many different plans had been proposed. The non-contributory plan was adopted because that was the plan favored by the Labor Party and because there was no need of immediate relief.

It was interesting to note from the aforementioned study that at that time about 1/5 of the whole population of the United Kingdom above the seventieth year were outright paupers when

---

[8] While this report is out of print, a copy of the original typed manuscript is in the author's personal files.

the act was passed. A pure insurance scheme such as our now U. S. Old Age & Survivor Insurance would have been of no avail to those who were already aged. Their time for paying contributions was past.

On the eve of World War I, the state of Wisconsin adopted a tentative plan for the support of the deserving poor. Since that time measures for federal aid to the states for public assistance have pushed aside this aspect of "deserving" poor. Old age assistance at the time of this writing is universally given to those in need without any regard as to whether the receiver is deserving. This change in public policy has given rise to some very distressing experience in this regard, and while public relief is an evidence of enlightened public policy, nevertheless for a time it began to take on the nature of a social disaster. Attempts were subsequently made to alleviate the abuses inherent in such a scheme. Nevertheless, the drain on public funds for public assistance reached staggering proportions. At the time of this writing (1968), "The War on Poverty" is designed to ameliorate this situation. However, this, too is a drain on public funds.

Prior to World War I, employers in this country evidenced much of the same characteristics as the employers of nineteenth century England. Although the industrial revolution came later, our U. S. industrialists and business executives were imbued with the philosophy of "laissez-faire" -- a philosophy implying that public authority should "let alone" economic enterprise. It can be recalled that these were the days of the Carnegies, Rockefellers, Harrimans, Andrew Mellons, Judge Garys and many others like them. Such industrialists have been referred to as "industrial barons," and "industrial empire builders." They were the men who were the product of their time, a period of industrial buccaneering when the individual employee did not get much consideration as a human being. The employee was only a worker, a "hired hand" in the economic grist-mill for the accumulation of wealth, or economic power, or both, for the "Masters of Industry."

It was the time of free immigration when countless numbers of the underprivileged of Europe were ready to accept the risks and potentialities of the New World. Workers were in ample supply. The long hours of work, prevalence of child labor, the accident and health hazards were such that, since competitive industry could not readily reform, it came to be recognized that it was imperative that public authority should be the agency or means to protect people at work so that the interests of society at large could be safe-guarded. In my own mind I am certain that the agitation of the Socialist philosophy had a telling impact.

In this pre-war setting—although Massachusetts and a few other eastern states had taken legislative steps to benefit employees—it was the state of Wisconsin that pioneered the modern concept of protective labor legislation with adequate enforcement powers and procedures. Reference has already been made concerning the workmen's compensation law of 1911. However, the most significant development to my mind was the enactment of the Wisconsin "Industrial Commission Law." This statute of historical significance established a Commission with quasi-judicial power to administer the laws enacted for the protection of employees. These statutes, which the Industrial Commission was established to enforce, comprised factory safety, workmen's compensation, child labor, hours of labor, wage legislation, regulation of private employment offices, apprenticeship, and many others.

Before the passage of the Industrial Commission law, what labor statutes existed were enforced either by a factory inspector or a bureau. In either case violators of the law were "brought to book" in the courts. This was obviously an ineffective way to assure compliance in a growing industrial society, in great contrast to the Commission form of administration. The following quotation from the statutes shows the wide scope of administrative authority with which the Commission was and is endowed.

The industrial commission shall have power, jurisdiction and authority:

(2) to administer and enforce, so far as not otherwise
provided for in the statutes, the laws relating to child
labor, laundries, stores, employment of females, licensed
occupations, school attendance, bakeries, employment
offices, intelligence offices and bureaus, manufacture of
cigars sweatshops, corn shredders, wood-sawing machines,
fire escapes and means of egress from buildings, scaffolds,
hoists, ladders and other matters relating to the erection,
repair, alteration or paining of buildings and structures, and
all other laws protecting the life, health, safety and welfare
of employees in employments and places of employment
and frequenters of places of employment.

(3) to *investigate*, ascertain, declare and prescribe what
safety devices, safeguards or other means or methods
of protection are best adapted to render the employees
of every employment and place of employment and
frequenters of every place of employment safe, and to
protect their welfare as *required by law or lawful orders,* and
to establish and maintain museums of safety and hygiene
in which shall be exhibited safety devices, safe-guards and
other means and methods for the protection of life, health,
safety and welfare of employees.*
*Wisconsin Statutes, Section 101.10 (2) (3).
(Italics, author's.)

On examination it can be seen that this is quite a departure
from a bureau of statistics, or a factory inspector, where it would
usually be necessary to await a complaint brought to the attention of the factory inspector from some individual aggrieved employee.

It is well to note here that the legislature lays down the
principles, the substantive law, but the Industrial Commission
determines the application of the law. For example, while the
legislature specifies that a place of employment must be safe, it

is certainly impossible for it to know exactly when and where in specific situations the conditions are in compliance with the principles of the safety requirement of the statutes. For this reason, it is necessary to have an administrative body with power to investigate, determine, and fix special rules and orders, so that the will of the legislative body can be carried out in practice.

In fixing these reasonable classifications and determining special and general orders for enforcement of the statutes, the commission first consults representatives of the industry or field of activity under its jurisdiction by setting up special committees representing the varied interests in the given situation. Later the determinations of the respective committees are subject to public hearings in different parts of the state, so that when the specific orders are subsequently promulgated by the commission they will represent the most authentic and effective regulations that can be devised. This method assures the cooperation of the majority of employers and results in an effective enforcement of the respective protective labor statutes, which are many, covering all aspects of the employer-employee working experience. As I commenced my graduate studies in 1912, four states—Wisconsin, Colorado, Ohio and New York—had embarked on this method of labor law administration. It was a matter of great interest and excitement among students. Today this type of labor law administration has become well nigh universal in this country. It is scarcely possible to over-emphasize the significance of this procedure for law enforcement.

The proponents of these modern labor protection statutes discovered that a law cannot be better than its administration. It is quite possible that a relatively poor law well enforced might prove to be superior to a good law inadequately or inefficiently enforced.

In a preceding paragraph I mentioned the influence of the Socialists. In recalling the fact that Wisconsin pioneered in modern protective labor legislation, it is well to remember some of the conditioning factors. At the beginning of the century, Milwaukee, Wisconsin, to my personal knowledge, had quite a constituency of German Socialists. Victor Berger, a native of Austria, was a Socialist member of the House of Representatives. He was the prime mover behind the *Milwaukee Leader*, which newspaper for many years was the voice of Wisconsin Socialists. While historically there was a long-standing cleavage in the Labor Movement between the Socialists and the Trade Unionists, or what in other language would be termed the "Political Actionists" and the "Economic Actionists," this was not so evident in Milwaukee. The Socialists were so much in the majority that any union man who aspired to be a leader was virtually compelled to declare himself a Socialist. Frank Weber, the organizer and many years the president of the Wisconsin Federation of Labor, was what was then classified as a Scientific Socialist. In conversing with him it would be hard to escape his aside, "Come the Revolution, we will do so and so." It would appear that he was committed to Marxism. Weber and his associates, however, were at heart good trade unionists, but their ideology was Socialism. Milwaukee had to my own knowledge three Socialist mayors covering most of the period from 1912 to the 1960s, except for the 12-year incumbency of Carl Zeidler.

The Roosevelt New Deal and the circumstances of World War II emasculated American Socialism. Many Socialists, such as Mayor Dan Hoan who was Milwaukee's Socialist mayor for 24 years, threw in their lot with the New Deal Democrats.

It seems that members of the general public whose attitudes were reflected in the legislation of the first decade of the century were more sensitive to the needs of the worker than were the employers of labor of that day, who were not yet ready to abandon the philosophy of "laissez-faire." There are still a few individuals who today have not seen fit to abandon it.

Before the turn of the century there had been a good deal of labor unrest and many outbreaks of industrial conflict. As an undergraduate I learned that in 1901 there was formed the National Civic Federation. The idea of this organization was to promote "trade agreements." At the time trade agreements meant agreements between employers and employees, which today are called "labor contracts." This apparently indicated that some farsighted industrialists and public-spirited citizens of the day became cognizant of the importance of arriving at a peaceable solution of industrial conflicts. However, it should be noted that as worthy as was the goal of the National Civic Federation, that of industrial peace, it was by no means the same thing as a realization of the need for protection of the individual workers. It was not in any sense an awakening to the necessity of recognizing what was needed to protect and to dignify the essential humanity of the workers as important members of our industrial society.

In other words, there is a difference between what steps may be taken to calm the "industrial storms," and what measures are invoked to dignify and embellish the lives of individual citizens who, by the conjuncture of circumstances, are destined to take their place in our society as employees, or industrial workers. At the beginning of this century, employers generally had not yet become conscious of the need to recognize and protect employees as fellow citizens and as dignified human beings. More protective legislation became a social necessity.

The first state efforts to regulate women's hours, child labor, and working conditions met with frustration. Employers of labor contested the legislation on the grounds that it interfered with freedom of contract and enjoyment of property rights guaranteed by the United States Constitution. As a consequence the courts first declared these laws unconstitutional. The Federal government tried to meet the needs of the time by the passage of statutes to regulate the employment of women and minors in industries engaged in interstate commerce. These, too, were held to be unconstitutional. The Supreme Court held that the Federal government did not have the power under our constitution to interfere in private industry, which power presumably came under the prerogative of the individual states.

On December 29, 1916 the same Bellafontaine, Ohio *Index Republican* which contained a write-up of my marriage, also contained an account of a meeting of the American Association for Labor Legislation (of which I was a member) at the Ohio State University. In this session, among other observations, John A. Voll, president of the Ohio Federation of Labor, declared:

> 'It is impossible to measure the brutalizing influence of laboring seven days a week. Social groups of all descriptions should work in union for this reform that means so much spiritually, mentally and physically to the human family.'

And he added:

> 'Profit, material welfare and interest must not be allowed to stand in the way of human progress and preservation of man's social soul and body.'

Another speaker, John A. Fitch, author of The Steel Workers, and editor of the Industrial department of 'The Survey,' in his address on 'One Day of Rest in Seven by State and Federal Legislation,' declared that

> 'Our campaign should be for a weekly rest day, not alone for the workers in the continuous industries, but for all workers in all industries.'

The Federal government did not acquire the constitutional right to regulate private industry until the year 1937. This came into being by court interpretation of the meaning of "interstate commerce" in the case of National Labor Relations Board vs. Jones & Laughlin Steel Corporation.

Not all legal theory postulated in the beginning of this republic in an agricultural society of 1789 could be expected to be

sacrosanct in the twentieth century, in a society which had become highly industrialized. Today we have hundreds of legislative enactments and administrative procedures that have been
validated by the courts under the doctrine of the "police power."
Those who construe the United States' constitution of 1789 as
adequate for all time are shocked by the manifold restrictions of
the present day, and view with alarm the encroachment of public
authority on what had been regarded as our fundamental individual right of personal freedom, contract, and property. However, well-informed, socially conscious citizens are compelled to
reason that individual rights must be exercised in the interest of
the public good. This is the basis of factory safety, regulations
of public utilities, use of highways, and all such activities that
impinge on the public safety, health and welfare. Of course, it
is possible that legislatures may be too zealous to limit personal
rights with a view to protecting the general welfare. However,
the other extreme, where self-interest would have full sway, is
also possible.

During the period that I was working on the fellowship with
the Industrial Commission of Wisconsin 1913-1914, the state legislature passed a minimum wage law for women and child labor.
It must be recalled that prior to World War I, immigration to
this country was open. Labor supply was really greater than the
demand. In women's occupations many times, wages were lower
than the cost of living. There was widespread public interest in
ameliorating this condition. Consequently, extensive investigations were made leading to legislative action. At this time eight
states passed minimum wages laws for women and minors.

This legislation interested me to the point of making a comparative analysis of these laws—a written descriptive analysis accompanied by a well-studied and executed comparative graphic
chart. It was suggested that I send this article and chart to the
editor of a noted publication on the subject of labor legislation.
This I did. I got no response until the material appeared in the

monthly bulletin in question. I was shocked to find this material under another person's name -- an associate in the office of the publication -- and the only reference to my effort was a statement that I had "assisted in preparing the chart." This was downright plagiarism.

That experience was a heart-breaker, but also a character revelation. Obvious, sometimes, are the ways of intellectuals whose egos must be satisfied at all costs. This is a pattern of exploitation of graduate students which is all too frequent.

The 1912 preamble of the constitution of the Industrial Workers of the World, which thrived in this country during the first decade of the century, states: "The working class and the employing class have nothing in common. There can be no peace so long as hunger and want are found among millions of working people and the few who make up the employing class have all the good things of life."

Another paragraph states: "It is the historic mission of the working class to do away with capitalism. The army of production must be organized not only for the everyday struggle of the capitalist, but also to carry on production; capitalism shall be overthrown." This movement, it must be recalled, existed in the United States before the time of the Russian Bolshevik Revolution of 1917.

The court's invention of the doctrine of the "police power" provided the way out of a dilemma. This doctrine refers to the exercise of public authority, that is, the power of the state. The court explained that the police power, not the same thing as military power, is that inherent power of the state to protect the health, safety and welfare of the citizens, an obligation which exists independent of, prior to, and in spite of, any written Constitution. If a statute can be shown to come under the authority of the police power, it will now be considered valid by the courts. It should be pointed out, of course, that it is the state which has this inherent power and not the Federal government. The Federal government is a government of delegated powers. In other words, it has such powers as were given it by the several states at the time of the establishment of the union. However, there are people today who think that the Federal government has some inherent power to protect the welfare of the Nation's citizens. They refer to the "Welfare clause" in the Preamble to the Constitution.

Since the onslaught of the Great Depression, legislatures and courts, because of the nature of a growing complex society, have rationalized a liberal interpretation of the Constitution, claiming that the circumstances of this jet age makes invalid some of the applications of the horse and buggy era. Most students of society in this space age see some justification for their view, while others are apprehensive of the ultimate effect if the process continues.

Since the passage of the Industrial Commission law in 1911, there has been a steady progression in the enactment and administration of measures aimed at protecting employees. In fact many of the developments have been not only to protect individual and groups as workers but to protect employees as citizens. It is not my purpose to analyze these statutes which have been a concomitant of my professional career, but to point out, to some extent, their evolution.

After the Wisconsin Factory Safety laws were enacted in 1911, a C. W. Price was employed by the Industrial Commission as a consultant to launch a drive for safety. He was borrowed from the International Harvester Company. He was working on the safety code while I myself was working with the Industrial Commission. The remarkable thing about the safety laws is the superb way in which the enforcement was launched. How did the Commission go about carrying out mandates of the legislators with respect to safety? That answer was built into the law by my major Professor John R. Commons, one of the original commissioners, who is referred to in Chapter III.

The highlight of the administrative process is the work of

special committees. In developing safety codes, representatives competent in their respective fields, as well as representatives of the public affected by the particular institution, comprise the membership of the committees. Those committees are permanent, although membership may change with time, as everything changes.

One of the first of these codes with which I came in contact was on safety in building construction. Representatives of the building industry and those directly affected by it were appointed on a building construction safety special committee. Hearings were held and proposals made and finally rules and orders were established by the Commission after they had been worked out by the interested parties. Obviously this made enforcement easier than any other process.

I myself was asked to make sketches of safety practices in building scaffolds, piling cement sacks, etc., which were used in the early stages of the building codes. Technological improvement, such as steel scaffolding, and mechanical material handling requires new and different safety practices, hence the periodic need to revise the codes with the aid of the industries' safety committee. So it goes for all the safety codes that have evolved during the past 40 years, and there are many.

Chapter V

INDUSTRIAL EDUCATION

Intelligent skilled labor is the foundation of economic progress.

Early in this century our manufacturers faced a labor crisis. The changed nature of immigration ceased to bring European trained craftsmen to this country. It was recognized that American industries had reaped where they had not sown. As suggested in the previous chapter, when the earlier supply of skilled men diminished by the erosion of time, there were none prepared to take their place. This situation became serious in the years immediately prior to World War I and the apprehension was intensified by the event of the War itself.

The only form of industrial education for centuries had been apprenticeship. Naturally a realization of the lack of the supply of skilled workmen necessitated the reexamination of the status of apprenticeship and what could be done to revive it, or at least to utilize it in American industry. Consequently some particular industries developed apprenticeship on an individual basis and then later sought to cooperate with other industries and with public authority. The goal was not only to develop apprenticeship, but also to explore other means of developing more efficient employees.

Thus apprenticeship proved to be the foundation stone of industrial education. In like manner industrial education was one of the mainspring of Personal Management. Personal management functions were later to be extended to cover such a wide range of human relations activities that they could be characterized only by the more comprehensive term "Industrial Relations."

Industrial education is a phenomenon of the twentieth century. As stated above, it became essential with the advent of World War I. The dignity of industrial workers is necessarily enhanced whenever there is emphasis on systematic education of employees. Much stress in recent years has been placed on the role of unions and unions' economic and political power in its relation to the improvement of industrial relations. Consequently, insufficient recognition has been given to the role of education on the improvement of working conditions and employment relations. Of course, organized labor has had an interest in vocational training as it has developed, but in the United States the labor movement in the past has not altogether appreciated a system of education for workers which would be different from that of other members of our society and have at times opposed it. In the early part of the nineteenth century, organized labor's interest in education arose out of the desire of the working man to have educational opportunity for his children as did the children of the professional men—doctors, lawyers, ministers, and the like. Remember, this land was heralded as the land of equality. The American worker seemed to shed the feudal concept of class consciousness. This is revealed by the tenacity with which labor clung so long to the traditional and formal educational pattern for working people, impractical as that was. Working men wanted the equal opportunity to become unequal. The skilled tradesman believed in apprenticeship, but other forms of vocational education were looked upon with suspicion by organized labor at the beginning of the century, because it ostensibly suggested inequality of educational opportunity for workers.

It was the employers in this century, in contrast to the labor unions, who first became interested in employee education and trade training. This was made imperative by the growth of the American economy, and the fact that at the same time, it was mainly unskilled and untrained workers who were immigrating into this country from the feudal lands of Southeast Europe. Getting trained workers became a serious problem. John B. Maling, giving an address before the twenty-ninth annual meeting of the Central Supply Association in the Drake Hotel, Chicago, October 4, 1923, made the following statement:

> Up to thirty odd years ago, when our great industries were expanding more rapidly than we could provide skilled labor for them it was the custom and the practice of the managers of the great industries to send their agents to Europe, and by promises of better wages and better living conditions to induce the best industrial workers of Western Europe to come to America. The cotton spinners of New England sent their agents to Manchester, and by such promises brought back the most skilled labor known in that industry. The silversmiths of Connecticut sent their agents to Birmingham and to Sheffield, and the ship builders along the Delaware sent their agents to Glasgow on the Clyde and to Belfast in Ireland and brought back the best ship workers the world ever knew. The silk manufacturers of Paterson and Allentown sent to France and brought back men who, through their ancestors, had been working in silk for a thousand years, and the German textile workers and the Scandinavian people were coming to our shores by millions. They were easily assimilated. They understood the philosophy of self-government. They were, in fact, almost the backbone of the development of our industrial life.

Then what happened?
At the time when Terence V. Powderly was just disappearing

over the horizon of events, and Samuel Gompers was earning his spurs, there was introduced into Congress a contract labor law. That contract labor law, as now, provided that any man living within the United States who would so much as write a letter to a man outside of the United States, offering him employment in this country should be fined or put in prison.

> The best labor of Western Europe, losing its assurances of place and position when it arrived here, preferred to remain where it was. Then the great steamship companies, foreign owned and controlled, knowing that, as the profits of a street car are in the straps, so the dividends in the transatlantic passenger trade were in the steerage. The Cunard Line, the Red Star Line, the Anchor Line, Allen Line, the North German Lloyd, the Hamburg American Line and the French and Italian Lines got together, seeking recompense for the loss of revenue. Caring nothing for the standard of citizenship in America, caring nothing about affairs in America, but only seeking to find the greatest mass of people that could be induced to be moved. In the Balkan countries, in southern Italy, around the head of the Adriatic and in southern Russia, they viewed millions of human beings seething and rebelling against the conditions in which they lived.

> They raised a great pool of money and had large posters printed and also printed pamphlets by the millions, in scores of languages, telling those people that this America was a land of milk and honey for them. They carpeted the valleys and they paneled the hillsides with those posters. They scattered those circulars to millions and they set in motion a tide which they kept up until they had landed more than ten millions from the poorest centers of that Old World upon the shores of America, bringing about the problems, civic, political, religious and social, which we are facing today. People untrained, untutored in

self-government, alien in spirit to our civilization, and that
is what we exchanged for the very cream of the industrial
talent of Europe when we permitted the labor unions to
put through Congress the contract labor law.[9]

Whether or not the contract labor law was responsible for
the shift in the character of our immigration, the facts were
that American industry could no longer rely on immigration
for its skilled labor. Before and during World War I, the European trained skilled workers were dying off. Some of the larger
manufacturing, merchandising, and railroad corporations felt
the necessity of setting up schooling facilities in their own establishments. Public education was academic in character and,
as suggested above, was the product of an ideal that all persons
should have the identical educational program. This, of course,
was manifestly impossible and equally undesirable, even under
an agrarian economy, much less in a growing industrial society.

The public schools attempted to overcome this practical
weakness by establishing programs of "manual training" in the
high schools. These programs now go under the designation of
"Industrial Arts." This, although desirable, was no answer to the
need for the education and training of industrial workers. There
were two reasons for this, one that the atmosphere of the school
lacked the conditioning factors of industry, and the other, the
fact that at the time, the students who attended high school
did not come from the economic stratum that furnished the
essential labor power for industry. Of course, the public schools
could not prepare young people for specific occupations in industry. Industrial leaders found it necessary to establish schools
in their own corporations. Later, as one would expect in this
connection, the industries decided it would be profitable to join

---

[9] "Man Management," American Management Association 1922-23-24, pp. 16-
18.

in these industrial education activities and learn from one another. Consequently, on January 24, 1913, the National Association of Corporation Schools was organized in New York City. In September, 1913, this Association held its first annual convention in Dayton, Ohio.

The spearhead of this organization was the New York Edison Company whose Mr. Hendershott and Mr. Arthur Williams "saw eye to eye" in getting together the leading corporations that had established schools or training centers within their establishments. In the discussion at the organization meeting of this association, it was apparent that these corporations which were to make up the National Association of Corporation Schools hoped their movement would have as one result the modification of public school education. They wanted the educational program of the public schools to be more helpful in preparing potential employees to fit into industrial and commercial employment.

Our society was moving away from an agricultural to an industrial economy, and it was clear that changes in our educational system were necessary and inevitable. Furthermore, the exigencies of World War I forced many considerations into the foreground. The need for improving productive efforts because of the necessities of war intensified the consideration of methods and procedures to make more efficient the output of American workers. It was realized however, that education *per se* was not sufficient to guarantee either the optimum or the maximum of production. It became apparent that much needed to be done to change the work environment; much needed to be done to improve relationships between supervisors and workmen. Much also had to be done to provide safe work places for manufacturing processes, to look after the ventilation and lighting, etc., as well as other considerations that have an impact on the employee's productive effort.

It seemed to me as a person involved in these issues at the

time, that the subjects considered in the realm of training, and what that implied in the broad concept, was the beginning or the foundation of what today we call "industrial relations."[10] Before World War I it could not be imagined what the development would be later in the 20's. There is no question that the requirements of the war helped to bring out some of these latent possibilities.

However, the state of Wisconsin took an advanced step before World War I. It passed a Continuation School Law in 1911 (to be discussed later) and at the same time enacted a statute to promote and regulate apprenticeship. The apprenticeship statute was replaced by another in 1915. This legislation pioneered the state supervisor of apprentices.

Before World War I there had been formed a Society for the Promotion of Industrial Education.[11] This society, together with other forces, was successful in conditioning public opinion, so that by 1917, the Congress of the United States, responding to the needs of the time, passed a vocational educational law that was known as the Smith-Hughes Law. This law made provision for appropriations to subsidize states that provided facilities for the training of vocational teachers and other services in order to meet the demands of the industrial education movement. This, too, was given emphasis by the requirements of the war effort. The statute, provided for a Board of Vocational Education for its administration. The first director of the board was Charles A. Prosser of Dunwoody Institute, Minneapolis. This law was designed to provide for the type of education that the public schools had hitherto failed to provide. Some argued that it was impossible for the established schools to afford the type of training required. The Smith-Hughes Law was a testimony of the gen-

---

[10] Discussed in Chapter VI

[11] The author was a member.

eral social and economic significance of this new and necessary facet of education.

It was not sufficient to rely on private enterprise to solve the problems due to inadequate public education, or to wait until more states followed the leadership of Wisconsin, Massachusetts, Connecticut and a few other states. The development of vocational education was needed on a national scale. This was particularly made manifest by the demands of industry brought about by expanding markets and the requirements of a nation engaged in a world struggle. The Federal Board of Vocational Education had the responsibility to allot sums of money to those states which established a plan of vocational education, which it could approve as conforming to the purpose of the statutes. Of course, it is the inevitable result of outside financial aid that the benefactor, in this case, the Federal Government, would exercise a heavy hand of control of the education. However, it would be imprudent to allot money to state agencies without a knowledge of how the money is to be spent or whether the results would conform to the standards set by the lawgivers. It is true that bureaucrats (not using the words with invidious implications) may sometimes think that their own conception of what should be done is superior to that of educators on the local scene, and as a consequence therefore, cause some resentment.

By 1917, the state of Wisconsin had made substantial headway and in many ways was further advanced in its philosophy and practice of industrial education than was envisioned in the Federal law. The appointed agent of the Federal board, when first examining the Wisconsin program to see if it was to be approved, seemed to be critical and to insist on procedures unacceptable to the Wisconsin educators. I, myself, was present, as a courtesy, at a meeting of the Wisconsin State Board of Vocational Education in 1917 in Milwaukee, when the Wisconsin Board of Vocational Education took the position that if they had to meet the specific requirements stipulated by the agents of the Federal board, they would rather not accept Federal aid. This was embarrassing to the representatives of the Federal Board. The chief spokesman was from the East with a background significantly only academic. However, rather than having to go back to Washington with an unsatisfactory report, he modified his view and finally accepted the Wisconsin plan as one meeting in principles the requirements of the Federal Board. After the passage of the Federal Vocational Education Law, the terms "industrial education" and "continuation school" were dropped and the term "vocational education" became the vogue. Obviously conditions in the several states varied. A preconceived plan to be accepted by all states alike is not always conducive to the best overall results.

Referring again to the National Association of Corporation Schools, it was evident to this body that it was necessary to obtain the cooperation and support of public educators. At the 1916 convention at Pittsburgh, Mr. James Roosevelt, chairman of the Association's Committee on Allied Institutions, reported on the character of its membership. This committee consisted of Mrs. Roy E. Fletcher, representing the National Federation of Women's Clubs; Mr. Alvin E. Dodd, representing the National Society for the Promotion of Industrial Education; Dr H. K. Hollingsworth, representing Columbia University; Dr. D. Lewis Ireton, representing the International Trade School Committee; and Dr. William R. Ettinger, representing the Vocational and Trade Schools. Indicating the importance of the N.S.P.I.E., the chairman stated:

> In certain respects the National Society for the Promotion
> of Industrial Education can be a particular aid to the allied
> committee, for as the name implies, it is a promotion
> society. Therefore, the society has certain machinery
> to help promote industrial education, which the other
> societies and associations do not possess. The society has
> already made two surveys for vocational education and
> has also taken an active interest in proposed vocational

> legislation in Washington. Therefore, it would seem that in
> many respects the Society for the Promotion of Industrial
> Education is the proper agency to do similar work for
> those other organizations which are unable or which
> consider themselves unable to do work of this kind.

This of course meant that the National Association of Corporation Schools needed the support of the public to further its objectives.

From the vantage point of the 1970's, it seems difficult to appreciate the vast changes that have occurred since the beginning of the century. No longer are we concerned with the continuation of the education of boys and girls who have gone into industry at the age of 14 years. Now, compulsory education has kept most youths in school up to the 18th year. Moreover, if they were not in school, it would be difficult now to find jobs for them. Whatever may be said of our educational system in this country, something has happened to result in the improvement of science and technology, such as to create in the new world the impact of another revolution, scientific in character, which has already surpassed anything experienced in the history of the human race.

When one looks back, it is evident that human nature is inherently conservative. It is difficult for humans to comprehend the possibilities or rather the concomitants of change. During the period of innovation, experimentation and development of programs, it would seem that the individuals involved seem to indicate little understanding of the relativity of ideas and programs. People tend to cling to ideas and methods which have constituted the mainspring of their own active years. New generations have new problems brought about by the circumstances of history. This fact seems to emphasize the futility of any generation of reformers taking themselves or their ideas too seriously. In the United States, we are a people of extremes. When we get an idea of a desirable goal, we go after it with a single mind, over-organize, and frequently do what is known in descriptive slang as "running it into the ground." If there is any doubt about this, one should encounter some of the animated discussions and messianic declamations of many of the proponents of particular solutions for social and economic problems, which one may encounter in many convention proceedings. One has to live and follow through on a pioneering movement, such as characterized the growth of vocational education, to get the full picture. It is true that it is exciting and exhilarating to see one's pet ideas and solutions being brought about, but it is disillusioning later to find, perhaps, that the results of clear thinking and penetrating analysis of the pioneers is dissipated in the self-seeking activities of the "band-wagon followers."

My close association with industrial and vocational education was due to the fact that it was my privilege and responsibility to be the first state supervisor of the first modern statute designed to promote and regulate apprentices in the skilled occupations. Many academics at the time were critical of apprenticeship. Some manual training instructors declared that any bright manual training pupil could learn the essentials of a mechanical trade in six months of school. Apprenticeship was obsolete, they said. Even the noted industrial educator, Charles S. Prosser, appointed first director of the Federal Board for Vocational Education, in an address before the American Vocational Education Convention in Indianapolis, which I attended, referred to apprenticeship as the "deadest cock in the pit." While very many educators and industrialists were extolling apprenticeship training, other educators could sabotage the effort due to personal convictions growing out of limited experience. Apprenticeship may have had a relative decline in importance since, but it still remains true that many skills and occupations can be learned only in the crucible of experience. Until some years after World War I, Wisconsin was the only state in the union with a modern, practical statute to govern apprenticeship, sponsored by both organized management and organized labor. Later, as we shall see, the Federal government became committed to the promotion of apprenticeship training. The Wisconsin apprenticeship plan prospered in the 1920's and attracted the attention of other states. Inquiries concerning the Wisconsin law came to the Industrial Commission of Wisconsin not only from other states bur also from foreign countries and provinces. Letters of inquiry came from what then appeared to be remote corners of the earth, the states of Central Asia, New Zealand and the Union of South Africa.

To illustrate how history can be determined by the unexpected, we can cite the effect of the New Deal of the 1930's, a derivative, or a consequence of the Great Depression of that period. The New Deal had a facet known as the National Youth Administration, which through deficit financing by the National Administration had millions of dollars at is disposal to foster schemes for the benefit of the youth. It provided an opportunity for students to earn money for education through make-work programs. It established and operated training programs on its own without considering those that were already established by the states themselves. Some of this training was erroneously called apprenticeship. It was a relief program operated directly from Washington, D.C.

The consequence for Wisconsin was a considerable embarrassment. This I learned from Dr. R. L. Cooley, the outstanding philosopher and administrator of vocational education who was the "father" of the Milwaukee Vocational School of world renown. He related the story to me personally. Although at the time I was a university professor and no longer supervisor of apprenticeship, Dr. Cooley assumed that I, because of my genuine interest in apprenticeship, would be concerned with the following information that he related to the effect that the National Youth Administration was wrecking our Wisconsin apprenticeship program, which we had been developing over a period of 20 years. He told me that he had complained to the National Administration in Washington. He was requested to present the situation to the President. The President, Franklin Delano Roosevelt, I was told, took in the situation and responded with the proposal in words like the following: "Why not have a Federal apprenticeship program?" Consequently, as one might suspect, there was soon formed in the Department of Labor, a Federal apprenticeship committee. Later this became the Bureau of Apprenticeship.

Dr. Cooley was asked to nominate a person to administer the Federal apprenticeship committee program. On this he conferred with me and discussed the person of William E. Patterson who was associated with the Milwaukee Vocational School and who had at one time been an assistant in the department of apprenticeship with the Industrial Commission of Wisconsin. Mr. Patterson had worked with me on several projects. Mr. Cooley thought "Pat" as he was called, would be a good candidate for the Federal post. I agreed. Recently, Pat had lost his only child, a boy of about two years old through drowning in an excavation with a residue of water, about a half block from his home. Under the circumstances a change of scenery and activity might be good for the bereaved father since it would help to take his mind off his tragedy. At any rate, W. E. Patterson was nominated and later appointed Director of the Federal Committee on Apprenticeship. He was well-qualified and undertook his new responsibility with the good wishes of his Wisconsin friends. Congress appropriated money for this project.

The idea at first was to assist the states in promoting and administering their own apprenticeship programs by furnishing added personnel to work with the state apprenticeship authorities. In 1935, I was asked along with some other people from different parts of the country to be a consultant to the Federal Committee on Apprenticeship. The Committee had drawn up a model bill with the expectation that the individual states would pass such a bill, thus establishing a state apprenticeship plan in line with that presented by the committee. This model bill embodied the principles of the substantive law pioneered by the Wisconsin legislature in 1915. However, there was one line of departure. The Wisconsin Industrial Commission was given power and authority to administer the law according to "the intent and purpose of the statute." The Industrial Commission of Wisconsin, as noted elsewhere in this work, enforced its legal responsibilities through the advice of those elements of the public affected by any specific piece of legislation. Selected representatives on a voluntary basis assist the commission in helping to determine orders and rules for the enforcement of the law. These become valid only after public hearings. This has been manifestly good and the Wisconsin administrative philosophy and practice has been very effective. The procedure for administration was not specified in the statutes themselves.

However, the model bill in question, drawn up by the Federal Committee on Apprenticeship, incorporated in its administrative procedure the experience of Wisconsin with the substantive law. This had the effect of making the method of administration appear to have the same importance as the substantive features of the law. What had happened was that the method of administration which we had developed in Wisconsin, which was not necessarily a part of the specific apprenticeship law, was taken over "lock, stock and barrel" and incorporated in the model bill which meant that the states which needed Federal support on apprenticeship would be expected to pass the model bill and be forced to accept the method of administration which it prescribed. It called for trade committee members from unions, whereas in Wisconsin we required committee members chosen from the respective trades which, of course, necessarily would include union men. However, the Wisconsin law did not raise the "red flag" for those employers who resented the dictation of unions on apprenticeship. As a consequence, it made cooperation easier, even if the end results were the same. It was good to press the states to pass apprenticeship legislation, but to require the same type of administrative procedure I thought to be a grave error. For instance, one state might elect to have the state board of vocational education as the administrator of the apprentice law, while another such as Wisconsin would designate the industrial commission or an independent agency. Then again, the model law had written into it the compulsion to have representatives of organized labor on the committees.

The emphasis was on the organization politically conceived rather than that there should be representatives of the trade skills involved, which as I have indicated, would have inevitably included representatives of organized labor. Prescribing methods of administration in the statute itself made it more difficult to persuade particular state legislatures to pass such a bill. The fact is that the committee had taken the Wisconsin administrative procedures and to a degree, made it an important end in itself, rather than to focus the language of the bill on the principles of apprenticeship. They should have left the determination of the methods of administration to local authority. When called to Washington in 1935 as a consultant, I tried to present my view but found that was not what was expected or desired. Finally, I determined that we were not called upon to consult but only to approve.

At that time, the Federal Committee on Apprenticeship started out with the idea of helping to facilitate the development of state apprenticeship programs, but as might be expected, it was not long before all the emphasis and propaganda were centered on the question of Federal participation in apprenticeship programs. In my book on apprenticeship published in 1932, I made the following statement: "Our government is one of enumerated powers and its framers fully intended to reserve to the states as many powers as possible. The sentiment with reference to the proposed child labor amendments and also the growing opposition to the increase of Federal control in state matters through appropriations for subsidies, suggest that it is beyond the range of probability that the states would permit a program dealing with such voluntary personal relations as are required by apprenticeship to be imposed by the Federal government".[12]

Time and circumstance seem to make fidelity to basic principles less important than political opportunism. In a conversation with William Patterson, the national director of apprenticeship in 1935, he spoke in high terms of my book on apprenticeship but with a reservation that he did not agree with me so far as my appraisal of Federal authority on apprenticeship was concerned. The wish was father to the thought. Mr. Patterson's view of course could be expected, since it is natural that an administrator would be anxious to see his power of dominion extended. However, at that time I was on sound grounds.

Nevertheless, the case of Jones & Laughlin Steel Corporation vs. NLRB in 1937 extended the concept of interstate commerce. The Fair Labor Standards Act, enforced according to the new definition of interstate commerce, opened the way for the inclusion of apprenticeship standards as coming under the domain of the Fair Labor Standards Act, hence under Federal Authority. However, results would have been practically the same anyway as the dispenser of monies is bound to determine the manner of their use. I have noticed in the trade literature the employers are requested to write to Washington to be informed on the Federal apprenticeship program. Not once have I seen a directive to the employers to write to their local state authorities concerning apprenticeship.

Apprenticeship involves personal relationships between apprentices and their employers. An apprentice is not an institution, unlike a trade union, which is. It would seem to me that as much local authority and initiative as possible would be better than long-range control from the outside. There is another

---

[12] *Apprenticeship: Principles, Relationships, Teachers.* McGraw-Hill Publishing Company, 1932.

factor involved and that is the maintenance of respect for local authority.

When it was my function to teach university students on the subject of protective labor legislation, I was appalled at the complete ignorance of the students with reference to the character of state and local governments. This was especially pointed during the years of the NYA, previously mentioned. The NYA as indicated earlier provided money to help young students. However, the checks, instead of being issued through local government units, came directly from the United States Treasury. This I thought was unfortunate. Instead of making good citizens who would first be conscious of, and have respect for, state and local government, they learned nothing of local government and cared less since their checks came from what has been called the "Great White Father" in Washington.

The so-called Federal apprenticeship plan was not generically Federal at all. It was the Wisconsin plan, developed over years of experience, which was lifted and adopted by the Federal apprenticeship authorities. The same basic principles of the apprenticeship administration were determined from scratch in Wisconsin between the years 1915-1930. A legitimate circumstance that made for a greater participation by the Federal government was the question of retraining or training of veterans after World War II. Many of these were brought under an apprenticeship arrangement and of course the Federal government, having priority on the matter of veterans, would naturally have a strong part to play in the apprenticeship arrangements for veterans. Theoretically these apprenticeship programs are still state programs and are dependent upon the state statutes to cover. However, the fact that the Federal government provides for agents to assist the states in their work and provides money to further the program means in the end that unless the state administrative agency is very strong, the Federal authorities run the show,

Speaking for the Wisconsin administrative plan, it should be born in mind, that when the law of 1915 was passed there was no enforcement agency set forth, other than the ordinary powers of the industrial commission established by the Industrial Commission Act of 1911. It was necessary as related in Chapter III to have an administrator on the Industrial Commission Staff to enforce or rather supervise operations under the law.[13] It was incumbent upon a person that had been given that authority to devise some means to accomplish the purposes of the statute.

It wasn't an accident that through civil service I was chosen from a long list of applicants, in as much as I had had apprenticeship training which covered a five-year period. Moreover I carried a union card and understood the psychology of the union men. Furthermore, I was a University graduate and had had three years of graduate study majoring in the field of labor economics. So naturally, it could be expected that when we set out to lay out plans for the enforcement of the law, it occurred to me that it would be good to have the support of organized labor, as well as some of the employers' associations. That I proceeded to obtain. It is understandable that those employers who would be dealt with first would be those with which I had had some experience or association—for example, building trades, and construction employers, the construction workers, plumbers, carpenters, and the like.

Therefore, I endeavored to organize not merely separate committees to work out some of these problems, but to win the support of organized groups, and therefore, to get these groups to voluntarily commit themselves in their various conventions. I don't think this idea had ever been initiated before. The fact that I had had this experience with the trade union membership gave me the entrée and an insight into what could be done in this connection. This was not a matter of politics; it was a matter of economics. Of course, it is well known that political entities

---

[13] Mentioned in Chapter III

endeavor to get the support of economic organizations. However, to get a private organization to commit itself to a program which is government sponsored and administered, at the time was something quite unique.

It should be recalled that before World War I, the status of organized labor was quite different to that which has prevailed since the passage of the Wagner Act of 1935. It is true that in a country like ours, we get impatient in our endeavor to extend to all states a particular program that is thought to be an "answer to a prayer." However, the results are not always what would be expected because we are likely to stifle innovation and encourage regimentation.

The development of vocational education in Wisconsin had its "birth pains." Naturally, the entrenched functionaries of formal education thought themselves competent to administer the new type of education, even though they had not shown a real appreciation of its need. Others thought that vocational education required separate administration. There was a good deal of controversy at the educational conventions concerning the "dual" school administration. Not all states followed the Wisconsin plan, which has functioned so well in our state. On occasion, even in Wisconsin, attempts have been made to bring vocational education under the auspices of the State Superintendent of Schools, but the state law-makers, no doubt out of concern for the political effects of union-labor opposition, so far have not seen fit to depart from the original method of administration.

Wisconsin law requires local boards of vocational and adult education to be constituted as follows: two persons to represent employer interest, two to represent labor or workers interest and the local superintendent of schools representing the interests of general education. The plan works well so far as my knowledge goes. Organized labor is strong for this plan and there is no likelihood of departure from it in principle so long as labor's voice is politically potent.

There has been one hurdle to overcome with reference to getting the proper acceptance of apprenticeship, that is the phenomenon of social snobbery. The idea seems to prevail that apprenticeship is an inferior form or design of education, that proper social standing is predicated on a college degree. What utter nonsense this has become!

An apprenticeship can become an extraordinary rewarding educational experience. The extent of the development of a person depends upon the individual apprentice himself. An apprenticeship experience under proper surveillance, combining practice and theory, may be much more significant for many, than the same amount of time spent in formal education. Apprenticeship has no mean heritage. I quote from Adam Smith from his *Wealth of Nations* of 1776, where he observes:

> The University of Smiths, the University of Taylors, etc., are expressions which we commonly meet with in the old charter of ancient towns. When those particular incorporations which are now peculiarly called universities were first established, the term of years in which it was necessary to study, in order to obtain a degree of Master of Arts, appears evidently to have been copied from the terms of apprenticeship in common trades, of which the incorporations were much more ancient. As to have wrought seven years under a master properly qualified was necessary in order to entitle any person to become a master, and to have himself apprenticed in a common trade; so to have studied seven years under a master properly qualified was necessary to entitle him to become a master, teacher, or doctor, (words anciently synonymous) in the liberal arts, and to have scholars or apprentices (words likewise originally synonymous) to study under him."[14]

---

[14] *An inquiry into the cause of the Wealth of Nations.* Adam Smith, Everyman Edition, Vol. 1, p. 108.

It is a well known fact that many captains of industry have served apprenticeships. As a matter of record, most of the major manufacturing institutions in the last century were founded by men who had served a trade apprenticeship. In Milwaukee, for example, the founders of the brewing industries were men who had served apprenticeships in their business: in the metal trades; Herman Vilter, founder of the Vilter Manufacturing Company, refrigerating machinery; Henry Harnisfager, crane manufacturing; Theodore Trecker, machine tools, A. O. Smith, manufacturer of pressure vessels and automobiles, frames, etc.; one could go on at great length. In recent years a Mr. Roberts, a former apprentice with the Allis-Chalmers Manufacturing Company, became its president. Immediately prior to World War II, these were the men still on the scene, and with other like individuals were the leaders of the industrial community. They were outstanding men with whom to do business.

Apprenticeship is a very fine "springboard" from which to rise. It is with great pity and economic handicap when present day popular opinion downgrades apprenticeship training. An apprentice who is an intelligent human being, if he elects to do so, may surpass the useful knowledge and experience of that of his counterpart who spends the same amount of time in formal education. This is obvious when so many students in colleges are there only because the parents have the notion that it provides higher social status. Youth has to gain maturity. What better way can that be achieved then by learning skills in industry and trade, while at the same time pursuing academic learning in evening schools, correspondence schools or other educational apparatus? In these days of the 40-hour work week, there is ample time for such means of acquiring learning. Our Continuing Educational Programs provide the means. This is a practical world and early encounter with reality is an advantage. It does not preclude a liberal education which any person with the necessary motivation can achieve on a self-help basis. After all, education is a personal thing and one must himself desire and apply himself to the task in order to obtain it. It is not something that can be handed down even while in the walls of the college or ivory tower.

I would not want to communicate the idea that I am an advocate of long apprenticeship. I recognize that at an earlier date boys started apprenticeships or other work jobs at the age of 14 years. At present time we require at least 16 years and usually 18 years of age before we allow people to go to work or enter an apprenticeship. That makes some differences. The apprentice today has a better schooling background than an apprentice would have in a former day. Apprenticeships must be tailored to suit the particular situation in the different trades and industries. Skilled occupations continue to go through changes because of the technological improvements, new materials, special tools and the like. Although apprenticeships may be shortened, still the fact remains that the best way to learn is by doing. You can't teach a person to swim until he has been in the water.

My conception of present day apprenticeship has been explained in the book I wrote on apprenticeship in 1932. In that book, I advocated apprenticeship which involves a learning period covering a number of skills in a particular industry or occupation, inferring that it was not the length of the time involved that was important, but the content that would go into the experience while the period of learning lasted.

The principles of apprenticeship have valid application in many ways other than in the trades. It can have a significant role in many professions. Furthermore when industry, business and medicine recruit students for "internships" it is a tacit acknowledgment of the value of learning by doing.

In the summer of 1906, prior to my entry into college, I was fascinated to learn a new program of education related to the principle of apprenticeship. While riding in the streetcar across the city of Cleveland to work one morning, I was reading the *Cleveland Plain Dealer* which carried an article about Dean

Herman Schneider of the University of Cincinnati and his program to have students alternate school and work experience. This intrigued me because it confirmed my belief that in the United States one did not have to "lose caste" by working one's way through school.

This plan initiated by the University of Cincinnati proved a marked success. The school takes the employer into partnership and recognizes the educational value of work. The school and the employer cooperate in the plan which is administered by the educational institution. It was called "Cooperative Education." It was adopted in subsequent years by many other educational institutions. After the First World War, one of those institutions was Marquette University, and of all things, it was I who became the coordinator of the Marquette University College of Engineering Cooperative Plan. In my book on apprenticeship mentioned above, I devoted two chapters to the administration of cooperative education, one of which was on the principles, and the other on the problems.[15]

How did I get into this experience? A faculty member of the College of Engineering had persuaded the Jesuit Regent of the College, Father John Kremer, that because of my state apprenticeship administrative experience I would be a proper person to "sell" and supervise cooperative students for Marquette. It was 1922, during the slack period of the first Post World War depression that I was approached about this position. I accepted the undertaking with the understanding that in addition I would teach principles of economics to the engineering students. This was essential to me because I could capitalize on my graduate work in economics. Therefore I began my association with Marquette University September 1, 1922 as Professor of Economics and Industrial Relations. The supervision of the co-op plan was

---

[15] Stewart Scrimshaw, *Apprenticeship - Principles, Relationship and Problems* (New York: McGraw Hill Co., 1932.)

my project from 1922 to 1928, after which I became a full-time academic professor until June of 1954.

This co-op experience was uphill work. Industry in those years was run by practical men, not many of whom had been the beneficiaries of higher education. Furthermore the product of the last 19th century immigration from South-Eastern Europe had not yet come into its own. There was a great deal of prejudice then concerning the product of Catholic schools. However, that made the challenge more engaging. Marquette's cooperative program had phenomenal success until, like a lot of other enterprises, it suffered with the onslaught of the Great Depression of the 1930's. Before the Depression we had over 300 cooperative students in Milwaukee industries, and Marquette was being solidly integrated into the Milwaukee industrial community. It has been a source of great satisfaction to see the products of the cooperative program become top managers in Wisconsin industry and business, both public and private. For me it has been hardly possible to go into an industrial establishment without being cordially received by a former cooperative engineering student, who subsequently rose to high responsibility and influence.

This cooperative educational venture was exactly what Marquette University needed at the time. It was a terrific lever for Marquette's progress. Incidentally it has been a great experience to have been associated with Marquette University "on the make," so to speak.

Since the great war, "industrial education has operated in reverse." American Industrial Management has appreciated the value of refresher courses and academic learning for its supervisory and professional personnel. As a consequence, management training centers have been brought into being all over industrial America. Executives may return to the ivory tower. Fortunately the lever works both ways. Practical experience is good to bring to the classroom, and the elements of the classroom are good to bring to experience.

In the 1970's, it is obvious that industry and education are partners and it appears to be imperative that that be so if we are to survive as a prosperous nation.

Chapter VI

PERSONNEL MANAGEMENT

*It is not what the law says we may not do, but what
the human reason and justice tells us we ought to do.*
Apology to Edmund Burke

In previous pages I have referred to the plight of industrial
workers during the latter part of the last century and the beginning of the new. As indicated in Chapter II, I learned a great
deal at that time concerning the labor conditions while an undergraduate student, and more while working at my trade in the
summer vacations. Working on new buildings for the rubber industry in Akron, Ohio and on "skyscrapers" in the city of Cleveland afforded quite an insight into practical working conditions.
Later after graduate school, visiting industrial establishments in
Wisconsin during the years 1915-1920 as the first State Supervisor
of Apprenticeship, it was easy to experience first-hand the "feel"
of the pre-War labor conditions and the psychology of management. It was plain to see that the "master and servant" relationship was not yet dead.

   In early industry, and extending a long way into the 19th century, the term "master and servant" prevailed, a "hang over" from
the feudal system and the agricultural economy. As the factory
system characterizes the economy, and as employees no longer
work directly under the personal direction of the owner, the

master and servant terminology begins to give way to that of "employer" and "employee."

The basic personnel functions of management were carried on by the foreman to whom was delegated the power to hire and fire. This was the situation that prevailed prior to World War I. At this time the characteristic attitude of the employing firm would be to think it unnecessary to consider personal wishes of the employees, either as individuals or as groups.

It was not considered fitting for owners and managers of industrial enterprises, many of whom regarded their workers as "servants," to consult them as to what the wages or conditions of work should be. As one employer from the South, on being asked by me why he couldn't confer with his workers concerning the terms of employment, answered with the air of one responding to a personal affront, "Sir, do you think I would consult my servants about the wages I should pay them?"

Wages were low, hours long, working conditions often times deplorable, and seldom, if ever, conducive to the health and welfare of the individual workers. Of course, American workers were not disposed to accept this situation, as we say, "lying down." Consequently, industrial strife was the order of the day. While the American worker was much better off than his European counterpart, he was a long way from realizing in the economic sphere what he was presumed to be the beneficiary of in the political sphere. He had much vaunted freedom and equality in the political realm, but no such freedom and equality in the realm of economics.

In the industrial literature of the day there was much said pro and con concerning "capital" and "labor." These were abstract terms. Capital conveyed the idea of the capitalist employer and Labor was the term used to identify workers, organized or unorganized. In these early years the term "employer" and "employee" were seldom used, if at all. Many places of employment advertised for additional help by signs on the employment office bulletin boards: "Hands Wanted."

Workers were generally termed laborers or servants. Even craftsmen in the public mind were classified as laborers. At all events, industrial workers of all descriptions were referred to as "labor" except those who were termed "bosses" or "masters." As indicated in Chapter IV, the *laissez faire* system of the nineteenth century was reaching an impasse, which, had it not been mitigated, might have invited revolution which could sweep away the good as well as the bad of our Western capitalism. There were, however, a few employers who sought to improve labor conditions by the introduction of employee welfare programs.

As an undergraduate, I had studied the welfare system which Robert Owen established in New Lenark, Scotland, a remarkable humanitarian venture familiar to all students of economic history and the social sciences. This had some impact on American industry in presenting a new concept of employee welfare. An early American welfare management effort was tried in the cotton mills of Lowell, Massachusetts.

The first of the American industrial establishments to embrace employee welfare which came to my attention as a student was the National Cash Register Company of Dayton, Ohio. Since I was in school in Delaware, Ohio, it was easy to become cognizant of such an enterprise relatively nearby. The National Cash Register Company revealed in one of their bulletins in the early days of their welfare work, that in 1892 cash registers worth over $50,000 were returned due to defective workmanship. It was then that the company decided to take some interest in the employee's welfare with a view to getting a better product. Welfare work apparently did bring results.

Welfare work was later developed by a number of other American industries. These early welfare projects were generally those that the owners or managers thought to have special merit. They were many times the application of ideas of the owners or managers, such as in one case, factory environment; another recreation activities; a third employee housing, etc. By implication, differing motives governed the introduction of welfare work. More on that subject later.

In the decade immediately prior to World War I, it was apparent that we were in transition from an agrarian to an industrial economy. American industry just grew up. To add insult to injury there was the immigration pattern referred to in the previous chapter. Immigration was practically unlimited. In that April day in 1906 when I myself immigrated into the United States, 12,000 people landed in New York. That is quite an addition to the labor supply for one day. In the decade 1901-1910 immigration had a peak of 8,795,386.[16]

Imagine workers having to compete in such a labor market. Labor conditions were so bad and general labor unrest was so pervading that journalistic reformers made great capital in exposing them in magazine articles. These journalists were called "Muckrakers."

American industry was crying for improvement. Industrial leaders were groping for solutions they were unable to realize. Experimentation with welfare work was hit and miss. Standard practice had not been achieved. However, things were moving. An engineer by the name of Frederick W. Taylor was promoting industrial efficiency. He thought his system would solve the labor problem as well as increase production. This efficiency movement began with Taylor in the 1890s and developed by him and his followers to become the vogue through the 1920s. The efficiency movement became the "Taylor System" and later "scientific management."

In my undergraduate days as an economics student, under Professor George Gorham Groat, who had written a book on problems of labor, my attention was called to an article in the *Outlook* magazine dealing with what was claimed as a new dis-

---

[16] World Almanac

covery which would solve the issues between capital and labor. This was as early as the year 1910. This new discovery was the "efficiency movement." This particular article told of Frank Gilbreth's notions of how scientific management could increase the productivity of the bricklayers. It involved motion study, special raised platforms to hold mortar and brick so that less skilled persons could place the bricks in such a way that the bricklayer would not have to turn over the bricks to find the proper face.

Since I, myself, was skilled in this particular trade, and was plying it to work my way through college, I was prone to be hypercritical of Gilbreth's findings, and indeed most of his theoretical presentations seemed unsuited to conditions where no two buildings were alike, and where changing weather conditions make it necessary for the mechanic to make new or different manifestations of his skill every day. Furthermore, I thought that there was nothing new about studying motions. The most skilled among workmen instinctively study motions. In fact, it used to be a sporting game to see how one trowel of mortar could spread for the greatest number of bricks. Some would spread for three bricks at a time, some for four, and some for five. However, there were natural limits. A spread for five bricks would require a larger trowel than a spread for three bricks and of course would require more energy to lift. Different mechanics would prove equally effective by different methods depending upon the individuals' preferences, adaptability and physical strength. However, the stopwatch technique was something new. Gilbreth's example of applying scientific management to the ancient "art" of bricklaying did not appear to me to be as valid as it would be in activities outside the realm of "art."

Of course, I was prejudiced. Gilbreth did contribute many efficiency methods which are now in use, but I very much doubt that bricklayers today lay any more bricks per day than they did before this scientific management. However, they could do eight hours work with greater ease. The significant thing to note is that this introduced me to the subject of "efficiency" or what became known later as scientific management. Scientific management was destined to usher in a new era of management technology, particularly in mechanized industry.

It has been stated above that "efficiency" was heralded as a solution for the labor question. Taylor recognized that the disputes between labor and management there was on the management side a desire to obtain "a fair day's work for a fair day's pay." On the other side of the union was the desire for "a fair day's pay for a fair day's work." The unsolved question was "What is a fair day's work?" The answer was to be found in scientific management enabling the worker to be more productive without extra physical exertion, through efficiency. In other words, it was presumed that a fair day's work was something that could definitely be determined.

Needless to say, this new cult of "efficiency" had many ramifications, but it did not solve the difference between "capital" and "labor." It is fair to say that scientific management has improved the conditions of labor in many ways, although many of these improvements have been mainly the by-products of the quest for increased efficiency in production. However, these still leave the problem of reconciling labor's demand for their share of the increasing national product.

In the years immediately preceding World War I, as well as in those years right after, what might be called the "efficiency movement" became a nation-wide obsession. It appears that the need for increasing production in the expanding market in the United States due to the growth of the population demanded improvement in industrial technology. The old systems of management that were prevalent in the small shops were no longer sufficient for the larger industries with power machines. However, the old-fashioned system of foremanship was not sufficient to bring the desired results. Therefore, the piecework differential wage system developed, an indirect way to accomplish what could not be obtained by direct methods. However, this scheme of things did not provide the entire answer that was necessary. Americans are prone to take up a new idea and carry it to extremes until the idea becomes deflated or is superseded by another new idea. In the final report of the United States Commission on Industrial Relations published in 1915, from page 225, we find this revealing statement:

> "Scientific management as a movement is cursed with fakirs. The great rewards which a few leaders in the movement have secured for their services have brought into the field a crowd of industrial "patent medicine men." The way is open to all. No standards or requirements, private or public, have been developed by the application of which the goats can be separated from the sheep. Employers have thus far proved credulous. Almost anyone can show the average manufacturing concern where it can make some improvements in its methods. So the scientific management shingles have gone up all over the country, the fakirs have gone into the shops, and in the name of scientific management have reaped temporary gains to the detriment of both the employers and the workers.
>
> Fake scientific management experts, however, are not alone responsible for the lack of training and intelligence which contributes to the diversity and immaturity of scientific management in practice and its failure to make good the labor claims of its most distinguished leaders. The fact is that on the whole, and barring some notable exceptions, the sponsors and adherents of scientific management— experts and employers alike—are profoundly ignorant of very much that concerns the broader humanitarian and social problems which it creates and involves, especially as these touch the character and welfare of labor."

Under such circumstances, naturally, labor looked askance at this efficiency movement.

Frederick Taylor himself presents his point of view in testifying before a Special House of Representatives Committee in the following statement:

> "The great revolution that takes place in the mental attitude of the two parties under scientific management is that both sides take their eyes off of the division of the surplus as the all-important mater, and together turn their attention toward increasing the size of the surplus until this surplus becomes so large that it is unnecessary to quarrel over how it shall be divided.[17]"

Taylor gives a fascinating exposition of Scientific Management at this hearing including the experience of Gilbreth and his wife in the application of scientific management to the ancient art of bricklaying, as already noted, as well as the broad application to industrial operations. It is good reading and a very enlightening insight into our American industrial evolution.

It is not my purpose to make an exposition or appraisal of scientific management but to record that the movement, particularly during the twenties, made a profound impact on American industry to the enhancement of our standards of living.

At first, as previously indicated, scientific management was opposed by union labor as a "speed-up system." This was no doubt brought about because of the activities of the efficiency charlatans and partly to the manifest emphasis on individual performance. This appeared to be inimical to the interest of groups of workers, because it made more difficult the organizing of unions and the functioning of collective bargaining.

At this point it should be recalled that these observations are predicated on the conditions of a free society, where individu-

---

[17] Bulletin of the Taylor Society, 1926, Vol. XI, No. 3 & 4, p. 104.

als offer their services voluntarily. Taylor was very cognizant of the fact that the crux of scientific management was the cooperation of the workers and the proper functioning of the human element.

On the 25th anniversary of the Taylor society, H. S. Persons wrote a treatise designed to summarize the achievement of scientific management. In this work, the author epitomized what was the synthesis of the work of the members of the Taylor Society by the statement of four basic principles. These principles I have presented to classes in both industrial management and personnel administration, as well as to business groups. I have found them very serviceable; although they are not quoted verbatim, they are as follows:

1. Fearless experimentation, in other words, research.

2. Determination of standards, that is, set specific goals of achievement.

3. Planning, that is, in order to achieve the standards.

4. Maintenance of standards.

To reiterate, there must first be a search for the facts; then second, a determination of what is to be achieved, quantitatively and qualitatively; third, there must be intelligent planning of methods to obtain the standards or goals to be reached; and fourth, there must be continuous striving to maintain the standards or goals which have been established.

In all productive enterprises it must be remembered that human effort is the *sine qua non* of efficiency. It just happens that human beings are not as consistent as machines. They are subject to many variations, and even with the more competent, performance may slump and mistakes may be made, moods may change, and motivations may be adversely affected. These phenomena of human nature can be treated in such a way as to minimize their deleterious effect on performance. When we refer to maintenance of standards, we have to keep in mind that any type of enterprise to be successful must be able to maintain an acceptable standard of the product or the service offered in the free market.

To maintain performance standards where human endeavor is concerned, it becomes necessary to obtain the services of competent people, to see that they are properly trained for, or adjusted to, their respective functions, that they are competently supervised, properly ordered and motivated.

Whatever had been said of "efficiency" before the breakout of World War I, became more pointed after our formal entry into the war in April, 1917. It is almost impossible to exaggerate the impact of that war on American industrial society. First of all, immigration was prevented by the conditions of war. Men were drafted for the Armed Services. Women were brought into war industries in unprecedented numbers. The demands of war production brought into focus outstanding problems to be faced by management. One of the chief of these, of course, was the problem of maintaining industrial manpower. Now the demand for labor was greater than the supply. Employers were in competition for productive labor. The demand for war material was a great challenge to industry. To keep employees on the job became an overriding necessity. As a consequence, any and all attempts at employee welfare designed to promote loyalty and efficiency came into the foreground. Public authority as well as private industry embarked upon programs of Americanization of foreigners, meaning recent European immigrants, so many of whom faced the language barrier. The state of Wisconsin had a model Americanization program in operation under the auspices of the University of Wisconsin Extension Division.

To replace ships destroyed by German submarines the United States government had a shipbuilding yard at Hog Island, Pennsylvania. I had the privilege of visiting this in 1918. It comprised several shipbuilding units. These were operated under the pressure of competition. Inducements were offered that ostensibly made it a game for ship construction units to see which could complete the building of a similar "Liberty Ship" in the shortest time. Workmen vied with each other to determine who could drive the greatest number of rivets in a given time, etc. The several units had their separate welfare programs for their respective crews. It was a spectacular enterprise, capitalizing on schemes of welfare and creation, which were enhanced by a spirit of patriotism that was inspiring to witness. Now we were really in a situation where industrial workers welfare was being taken into account as never before.

During the early part of 1917 while visiting Boston, Mass., I made contact with an executive of the William Filene Store. This store had a nationwide reputation for enlightened treatment of its employees. I remember asking this person what his particular function was. He said "personnel." That sounded like a new word to me. I think that was the first time I had heard the expression which was then just coming into use.

When the military deal with war material, they call it material, and the labor power which they require to use this material is designated by them as "personnel." We can give the military credit for the popularization of the concept of personnel. The war industries caught on to the term which soon became a fact of life in our post-war development. It is strange to contemplate that years before this war in my contact with industry I had encountered the terms "workers," "help," "hands," "laborers," "mechanics," etc., but not once, the term "personnel."

Following the armistice of November, 1918 the United States experienced a period of fast-rising prices—a very pronounced inflation. During the War the government had issued "Liberty Bonds" to raise money for the war effort. These bonds were negotiable. In effect, the citizen who bought bonds loaned his cash to the government to purchase the sinews of war. However, he could use these bonds, discounted of course, to go into the market and compete with his own government for the same goods and services. Moreover, business encouraged bond holders to take advantage of their negotiability to make purchases with them. This, of course, increased the money supply relative to the available goods and brought about the pronounced post-war inflation.

It was my lot in 1919 in the City of Madison, Wis., to learn at first hand what this inflation meant. Early in the year 1919 my wife and I decided to build a home. We were able through the good services of Dr. Richard T. Ely, the renowned economic professor of the University of Wisconsin, to obtain a desirable spot on University Heights. The lot was purchased from Belshazer Meyer who was chairman of the Interstate Commerce Commission, and one-time professor at the University of Wisconsin. Dr. Ely was very much interested in land economics. We were fortunate to get his good advice to the effect that it was better to build a modest house on a valuable lot than to build a valuable house on a "cheap lot."

The reason we were intent on building was the fact that I had the energy, "know how" and skill to build a house myself, and wanted to prove it.

I applied for a building loan from the Madison Building Loan Co. and was turned down. I was informed that this was not the proper time to build. Being anxious to go ahead and being sure of myself, I applied for a mortgage from the Wisconsin Building and Loan Co. in Milwaukee. This application was approved. In the early spring of 1919 I began house building operations. I was my own architect. I hired a man with a horse-operated scoop to dig out the basement. With a local brick supply I built up the basement 12" brick walls, with a 2" air space in the walls for insulation.

With the help of a skilled carpenter who had been taking graduate work in Industrial Arts in the University of Wisconsin, we negotiated for material for the superstructure. All seemed to go well, except that we found it very difficult to get deliveries on time. I learned that the advantages of low competitive prices are of little value if deliveries are delayed, particularly in a period of rising prices. Wooden lath for plaster quadrupled in price. I had ordered two carloads of bricks early in the season but they were not delivered until after the end of the summer and only then after I had threatened to sue the supplier in a court of law.

In this period the demand for products was greater than the capacity to supply. Everybody seemed to be trying to "beat the other fellow" in getting deliveries. Many, too many, people placed duplicate orders for the same things in different firms. This added insult to injury. Bribery in the brickyards and railroad yards and with other suppliers was widespread. The carloads of bricks I was supposed to get at a certain time and at a certain price, had to stand aside because the supplier was able to capitalize on higher prices, or be influenced by generous gratuities.

I hired a union bricklayer to help me after my vacation time had expired. In a short time union bricklayers wages rose from 55 cents to 75 cents per hour.

Since my face brick arrived after the end of the summer season, it began to look as though I would not be closed in for the winter. However, I was a union craftsman, and the members of my union honored a tradition that a member of the craft, in building a home, should receive the donation of a day's work from the other members of the craft. Without solicitation the union members came out on Saturday afternoons and Sundays to see that I got closed in "before the snow flies."

The house was a brick veneer Colonial design with brick quoins (blocked to resemble corner stones), chimney at each end and three fireplaces of my own handiwork.

As recounted in Chapter VIII, in April, 1920, I was persuaded to change my occupation. I resigned from the position of State Supervisor of Apprenticeship and accepted an appointment as manager of industrial relations or personnel manager with the

Kearney-Trecker Corporation of Milwaukee, manufacturers of milling machines. It was a pioneering assignment. In a way I had to cut out my own sphere, supervising employment, devising re-cord forms, acting as safety inspector, being responsible for ap-prenticeship, supervision of first aid and medical case services, and community relations and the like.

Like most personnel functionaries of the time, I had to practice diplomatic skill to avoid unnecessary friction with the production executives whose prerogatives were inevitably chal-lenged in some areas. An important aspect of this new job was to be sure that no state statutes or state government regulations affecting employment, and safety, etc., were violated. During this period the most difficult problem was that of "labor turnover." I suppose never in our history was there a comparable period when employees changed jobs with such impunity. Employers through their associations were apprised of the great expense of hiring, training and fitting of new employees to replace those who would quit.

In a short period of time I joined the Milwaukee Employ-ment Managers Association, organized in 1919. I was an indus-trial "personnel manager," the first and only one in the city, and what was more significant, the only college graduate in such a po-sition, and certainly the only such functionary with three years of graduate study in economics and labor problems. Of course, I was received with mixed feelings. Some members were com-plimented by my coming in with them, others were jealous and contemptuous. This was something they said was for "practical men, not for college men."

At the time, I was well versed in labor legislation. I was in-duced to discuss "protective labor laws" at a monthly meeting. I gave a rationalization for such protective legislation. With this, "I got my foot in," so to speak. The next day I was represented as a socialist, etc. A socialist at that time as a personnel man-ager would be an anathema to industrialists. Fortunately, my new employer, who got the report, and who had known me for five years, did not believe the accusations. If he had I would have been out.

This Employment Managers Association, in a way, revealed the signs of the times by the very fact of its recent existence. This organization consisting of men only was, four years later, reconstituted as the Industrial Relations Association of Wisconsin, to include industrial nurses and any other individuals, men or women, engaged in any phase of industrial relations.

Welfare programs and personnel functions were at first indistinguishable. The National Association of Corporation Schools (a forerunner of the American Management Association) of which I was a member, published in its July bulletin in 1920 what was at the time considered to be the activities of the personnel department. The outline is on the following page.

From this outline, it can be seen that big industry (class A membership in the association) was going overboard in its endeavor to keep employees satisfied and on the Job.

CLASSIFIED PERSONNEL ACTIVITIES

1. Employee Representation in Management

(a) Shop Committee

(b) Employer's Unions

(c) Trade Union Representation

(d) Welfare Committee

(e) Federal Plan

(1) House, Senate and Cabinet

(2) Joint Council

2. Employment

(a) Psychological Tests

(b) Trade or other Tests

(c) Job Analysis

(d) Attendance Records

3. Educational and Training

(a) Corporation School

(1) Training for Specific Jobs

(2) Apprenticeship Courses

(3) Courses for Foreman

(4) General Educational Courses

(b) Cooperating with Public Schools & other Educational Institutions

(c) Library

(d) Inspection Trips

(e) Correspondence Method

(f) Conference Method

(g) Motion Pictures

(h) Americanization

(i) Employees' Personal Records

(j) Promotions and Demotions

(k) Wage Assignments

(l) Foreman Training

4. Safety

(a) Sanitation

(b) Hygiene

(c) Ventilation

(d) Illumination

(e) Accident Prevention

(1) Covering of Dangerous Machinery

(2) Posting Placards

(3) Training for Safety

(4) Fire Protection

(5) Other Preventive Measures

5. Health Activities

(a) Hospital

(b) Physical Examinations

(c) Dispensaries

(d) Infirmaries

(e) First Aid

(f) Physician

(g) Nurse

(h) Visiting Nurse

(i) Medical Advice

(j) Dental Clinic

(k) Compensation Department

6. Thrift

(a) Stock Ownership by Employee

(b) Other Profit-Sharing Plans

(c) Building and Loan Associations

(d) Other Loan Associations

(e) Pension or Service Annuity Plans

(f) Insurance Plans (including Group Insurance)

(g) Benevolent Association (including sick and death benefit plans)

(h) Bonus Systems

(i) Safe Deposit Vaults

(j) Investment Funds

(k) Continuous Service Organizations

(l) Vacation Funds

(m) Savings Banks

(n) Cooperative Stores

(o) Housing

(p) Suggestions

7. Company Restaurants

8. Musical Activities

(a) Company Band

(b) Company Orchestra

(c) Choral Societies

9. Welfare

(a) Athletics

(b) Theatricals

(c) Rest Rooms

(d) Boy Scouts

(e) Campfire Girls

(f) Women's Clubs

(g) Girls' Clubs

(h) Mens' Clubs

(i) Boys' Clubs

(j) Employees' Gardens

(k) Legal Aid

(l) Research

(m) Recreation

(n) Noon Hour Activities

(o) Country Club

(p) Dormitory

(q) Summer Camps

(r) Vacation Resort

(s) Sewing Classes

(t) Cooking Classes

(u) Nursing Classes

10. House Organs or Company Paper

As the year 1920 proceeded, inflation was getting out of hand. As soon as the buyers with multiple orders got a delivery from one seller, they would cancel the contracts entered into with other suppliers. In 1920, the cancellation of contracts became a national disgrace. By the middle of the summer of 1920 the bottom dropped out of business, and the first post-war depression was a sobering fact.

This depression was short but very severe. It revealed a fundamental change in the nature of the American economy. It dramatically accentuated the fact that the United States was no longer a nation characterized as a agricultural economy, but had become industrialized

When industrial activity slackened it meant unemployment and deprivation which, for the individual, could not be mitigated without the risk of losing self-respect. The circumstance was a shock. It was obvious that workers no longer had the soil to fall back upon. We were becoming highly urbanized. When there was no money coming in for rent and goods, it was imperative to receive help from relatives and friends or to depend upon public charity. This was painful, for many who had self-respect and were willing to work found themselves stranded through no fault of their own. At this juncture began serious public discussion of the subject of unemployment insurance which was to become a legal fact in Wisconsin in January 28, 1932, and in the nation on August 14, 1933.

Reference was made earlier concerning the development of welfare work and its incorporation with what was classified as personnel functions. In the early twenties, the security of personnel managers was precarious. Not even personnel directors can work miracles. In any event, personnel departments for the most part at this time were on a trial basis. Unfortunately some of the earlier personnel men were not sufficiently trained for the responsibilities inherent in the job. Many so called personnel directors were nothing more than glorified employment managers.

On joining the Milwaukee Employment Managers Association, early in 1920, I was informed that employment management was no function for a college man who is a theorist, but a job for practical men. It happened that I myself was the first college man in Milwaukee hired as an Industrial Personnel Director. At the time, line management was loath to trust the handling of employee relations to men of the new personnel department. Therefore, personnel men often had difficulty getting established.

To express the situation in another way, personnel men in the early twenties had an uphill task. One of the reasons for the new function of personnel management was the reduction of labor turnover. In the years that followed the first World War, the cost of labor turnover was an item of great concern to American employers. The personnel department was presumed to solve this problem. As a consequence, at personnel conferences and discussions, the theme of how to prevent "labor turnover" seemed to be the paramount consideration. This theme, in time, like the fetish of the pre-World War "efficiency," became less important and of little interest after the economic post-war Depression of the 1930s.

Later when personnel management had shed a lot of the paternalistic welfare activities, the union came to accept personnel departments as part of the facts of industrial life. Personnel management thrived through the boom of the 1920s until the Great Depression, when the Depression caused many personnel men to lose their jobs. It is significant that the agencies of Franklin Delano Roosevelt's New Deal used numbers of them to great advantage.

In spite of the Depression, personnel departments and personnel techniques had become a necessary facet of business and industrial management. The increase in protective labor legislation involving matters of employee safety, workmen's compensation, child labor legislation, women's hours, minimum wage law,

accident reports, employment statistics, etc. made the central-
ized control of matters affecting the labor force an absolute necessity.

After the onset of this depression, during the 1921 state legislative session, I was asked to serve on the Milwaukee Metal
Trades Association Legislative committee, also the Legislative
Committee of the Milwaukee Association of Commerce. Then
later, in spite of other responsibilities I had undertaken, I nevertheless continued as manager of industrial relations, on a part-
time basis, with the Kearney and Trecker Corp., until the middle
of 1928. This connection made it possible for me to be cognizant
of the developments of personnel management in the twenties.

Business picked up in 1922 and a business boom ensued. Now
employers who had fired their personnel managers and abolished
their personnel departments were finding it necessary to reestab-
lish them. Welfare work *per se* smacked of too much paternalism
for native American workmen and organized labor opposed it.
They assumed that employee welfare programs were intended to
discourage workers from joining unions. Indeed, in many cases
it was true.

At the regular meetings of the Wisconsin Industrial Relations
Association, members discussed and compared with each other
their respective firm's experience with the turnover of the labor
force. It seemed at times that all the other aspects of personnel management were insignificant compared with the problem
of labor turnover. Some personnel men claimed that the reduction of labor turnover was the main object of personnel activities—the reason for existence of the personnel department. The
fallacy of this position became obvious to me when I studied
English industrial relations, on the spot, in the summer of 1926.
Economic conditions were not too good for the British in 1926;
consequently employees, as might be expected, held on to their
jobs. It was obvious to me that the elimination of labor turnover
could not be the chief rationale for the personnel department

—that other considerations were more important, and that a degree of labor turnover was a healthy sign of a free society.

Of course, personnel men did gather in the 1920's to discuss many other phases of employment relations. Programs were initiated to thrash out some semblance of standard practice on such subjects, for example, as employee "induction," how to prepare and place new employees, the problem of discipline, the formulation of Plant Rules, the proper procedure in separation (that is, techniques of lay-offs), problems of safety and accident prevention, and how to deal with the problem of absenteeism, etc. Then there were sessions dealing with matters of administrative policy. What administrative powers should a personnel director have? What is his relation to the line organization? These and other questions were thrashed out over the years until it became established that the personnel department and the personnel director should function as a service to the line organization.

Earlier in this chapter I referred to the enlightened attitude of the National Cash Register Company of Dayton, Ohio. It was John H. Patterson of the National Cash Register Co. who gave the address of welcome to the members of the first convention of the National Association of Corporation Schools meeting in Dayton, Ohio, 1913. In Chapter V on the subject of industrial education I had occasion to refer to the activities of that association. However, it is of interest at this point to relate how initial industrial efforts at joint action to educate industrial employees evolved later into a full fledged movement to improve employment practices and industrial relations generally until "personnel management" became an accepted industrial and business institution.

From 1913 to 1922, the National Association of Corporation Schools of which I was a member carried the ball for the emphasis on the "human factor" in commerce and industry. When experience showed that the greater percentage of training must take place on the job, this brought line management into the industrial relations picture. This organization came into being due to the pressures of war-time industry as the National Employment Managers Association, later called the Industrial Relations Association of America. This association and the National Association of Corporation Schools combined as the National Personnel Association. In 1923 the name was changed again to the American Management Association. Its publications and periodic seminars have been influential.

Photographs of Stewart Scrimshaw

Approximately age 25

Stewart (left) visiting the UK in 1926 (with a brother)

Approximately age 40

Fernwood and Stewart at a formal occasion

Fern and Stewart in Northern Wisconisn,1972

In his study, Wauwatosa, Wisconsin

Preparing for Marquette commencement in 1951. On table is a photo of son Norman, killed in France with General Patton's army in 1944.

As student advisor

In his boat - Three Lakes, Wisconsin

Stewart and Fernwood in Wauwatosa home

Fernwood and Stewart

Chapter VII

LABOR RELATIONS: EXPERIENCE WITH
THE UNIONS AND THE LAWMAKERS

*Freedom requires restraint; and Privilege
demands responsibility.*

In November, 1962, I received an invitation from the University of Illinois to join in the celebration of a dream which had become a reality – the completion of a new building to house the Labor and Industrial Relations Institute. It appears that with the combined financial support of the Illinois A. F. L., and C. I. O., the union membership, the state legislature, and the University, this noteworthy achievement came to pass. At the dedication the University president stated to the effect that the charter of the land grant colleges committed the University to the goal of serving **all** the people. Since the professions and the arts were provided for, as well as the interests of agriculture, it was now an obligation of the University to set up and maintain educational and research facilities to serve the interests of labor. This enterprise at this university similar to that of some other leading institutions such as Princeton, Cornell, California and others is a tacit reminder of the evolution of the institutional character of the present day labor force.

During the time the individual labor contract prevailed, the universities could do little more than incorporate the study of labor as a factor of production. Needless to say, this was very much in the abstract. Some universities extended the study to embrace protective labor legislation, which is designed to protect workers as individual citizens. However, when later laws were enacted to encourage and protect <u>collective</u> labor contracts, the institutional character of labor became a very important aspect of economic life. It is this fact that has led institutions of higher learning to become involved with problems not merely of labor, but of <u>organized</u> labor. The character and behavior of these institutions of labor have a profound effect on the fortunes for good or ill of our whole society.

In the 1920's and earlier, schools and colleges shied away form labor courses in the main because they developed controversy. This was even true in some cases with reference to courses in economics. Labor leaders and employers would not always agree with the information given, or the views taken with respect to the proper distribution of the national income. The university with which I myself was associated offered in this connection nothing more than a course in Labor Economics, or Labor Problems. It dealt with the problems of the labor force made up of individuals. It would not have done at that time to discuss collective bargaining. As a matter of record we had a distinguished Professor of Sociology in the University who suggested before a group that the only way employees could improve their situation was to organize. This statement aroused the wrath of some local industrialists who were employing the College of Engineering Co-op students for whom I was responsible. These employees made me the instrument to communicate to the university authorities that they regarded the conduct of this professor as hostile to their interests. No more needs to be said.

Another episode will serve to highlight the employers' emotions concerning unions in the 1920s. In the year 1924, I was instrumental in the establishment of systems of sequential courses in the Milwaukee Continuation School. Furthermore, I participated in this enterprise (related in more detail in another connection) to the extent of teaching a course in Labor History. I am sure this was a pioneering experience so far as any tax supported evening school in a metropolitan area is concerned. This course had not proceeded very far when I was surprised by a visitor from a large public utility. This visitor was the firm's educational director who had been sent by the president to protest that I had told students, some of whom worked for the utility in question, that organized labor's first goal in this country was to establish free public education, and that the unions had been one of the main forces in securing such a constitutional guarantee in the respective state constitutions as the new states were brought into the Union. Indeed, this was strong union objective taking form about the year 1827. I was asked why I told such things to my students? It was a disturbing factor! Was it really true?

I had to inform my visitor to communicate to his boss that I myself did not make the history, therefore, the objection should not be to me, but to the record. I mention the above to indicate how jittery employers felt with respect to unions in the twenties.

The purpose of what I have related above is to highlight the fact that no longer does a union represent a group of workers who have chosen a spokesman to negotiate with the employer for them on an informal basis. Today, these unions are legal institutions with strong economic, social and political implications, and their character and behavior have a very profound impact on the whole society.

How did organized labor become so significant? There are, of course, many reasons. I will relate what I consider to be some of the more significant. First of all, I would give the circumstances of World War I. To get the full cooperation of labor in war production, organized labor, which embraces considerable levels of skill, needed to be recognized and satisfied. President Woodrow Wilson appointed a War Labor Board which included in its membership five members chosen by employers associations and five members chosen by the A. F. L. Each group appointed a member who was presumed to be a public representative. It is interesting to note that Samuel Gompers, president of the American Federation of Labor, and Bernard Baruch, the New York financier, were on this board.

The unions were granted security for the duration of the War; this enhanced their status. Incidentally, I can say as an interested observer during those years, the cooperation of union workers of all types as well as other sections of the population was inspiring to behold. So far as I know, never before or since was the country so united and the citizens so cooperative. Of course we can discount the efforts of the pro-Germans in some of our cities who were guided by the illusory objectives of the Pan Germans and their Steuben Societies.

The demands of the war raised havoc with the railroads. Shipments of war material glutted our Eastern sea ports, so that the railway industry—then organized into many independent units—could not meet the challenge of the war. Consequently, in the national emergency Woodrow Wilson caused the government to take over, and manage the operation of the railroads. The railroad unions were demanding an eight-hour day. This was granted by the administration. This was the first direct government concession to organized labor. In 1920, the roads were returned to their private owners.

As a second reason for the growth in stature of organized labor I would place the passage of the immigration quota law of 1920 with its subsequent amendments. During the years just before the war the union's members had to meet the competition, or the potential competition, of the new arrivals to these shores. European immigration also brought ideological confusion among American unionists. A restriction of immigrants would make it easier for labor unions to solidify their gains, and enhance their effectiveness in dealing with public authority as well as to make a more favorable impact on public opinion. The immigration act had the effect of limiting labor supply and increasing labor's bargaining power.

As a third factor helping to elevate unions to the status of official partners in economic enterprise I would place the Railway Labor Act of 1926. It is profitable to explore the early government action with respect to organized labor on the railroads, because of its influence on succeeding legislation, and because it is evidence that union labor had received official public recognition.

To fully appreciate the Railway Labor Act from the point of view I have indicated, I would like first to make some observations of its antecedents. The Sherman Anti-Trust Act of 1890 states in Section 1

> Every contract, combination in the form of a trust or otherwise or conspiracy, in restraint of trade or commerce among the several states or with foreign nations, is hereby declared to be illegal. Every person who shall make any such contract or engage in any such combination or conspiracy shall be guilty of a misdemeanor.

Soon after the passage of this act there was a bitter controversy as to whether Congress intended the law to apply to organized labor. The courts felt compelled to follow the language of the law which included the words "any person." Several famous cases involving union labor came before the court, and the results proved inimical to interests of organized labor.[18]

Following the decision in Loewe vs. Lawler in the Banbury Hatters case[19] which rendered a judgment against the union for $252,000 (triple damages), organized labor put on a spirited cam-

---

[18] United States vs. Workingmen's Amalgamated Council of New York. Gompers vs. Buck Stove and Range Co. (1911) 221. U.S. 418.

[19] Loewe vs. Lawler (1908) 208. U.S. 274.

paign to have the law changed. However, it was not until the year 1914 that Congress passed the Clayton Act which stated, "Labor is not a commodity," and not an article of commerce, hence was not subject to action under the Anti-Trust Act.

The passage of this act was hailed by the labor chiefs as labor's Magna Carta. I remember the enthusiasm of labor's acclaim. Their enthusiasm for this "great charter" was short lived. The courts continued to make use of the injunction, and the unions still found themselves relatively at a legal disadvantage. The Clayton Act gave little relief from legal attack. These court injunctions became an effective defense weapon of the employers who opposed labor unions if indeed it were not a counter-offensive weapon of hostile employers. Again the unions carried a great campaign for relief from the frustration they suffered due to the issuance of injunctions.

The propaganda of the unions, aided and abetted by such noteworthy public personages as U.S. Senator Robert M. La-Follette and former President Theodore Roosevelt, succeeded in educating public opinion, with the result that during the Hoover administration the Federal Anti-Injunction Act of 1932 was passed, more generally known as the Norris LaGuardia Act.

It is this statute which, I think, more than any other could be termed organized labor's "Magna Carta." It "called off the dogs," so to speak, that attacked union organizers. This law not only limited the issuance of injunctions in labor disputes but it also gave a definition of a "labor dispute" which was new and designed to protect labor organizers.

To illustrate the meaning of the above, Child's Restaurant in Milwaukee, Wisconsin, functioning normally with good relations between the company and the employees, I think it was in 1934, was approached by an organizer from the East who requested the management to sign an agreement with the union he represented. Neither the management nor its employees was interested in the proposal. As a consequence this organizer from another state had pickets planted outside the restaurant to advertise that the management was unfair to organized labor. An attempt was made by the employer to stop this picketing by an injunction. However, because of the Federal and state anti-injunction laws, and particularly because of their broad definition of a labor dispute, the injunction was invalid. It can readily be seen that this situation would be a boon to organizers.

This broad definition of a labor dispute was destined to become of greater significance after the passage of subsequent labor relations statutes to be mentioned later.

The law furthermore forbade the Federal courts to enforce the "Yellow Dog" contract, therefore made it ostensibly illegal. Notwithstanding the significance of the above provisions, there is still another feature of this law, which seems to me to be very important. When I mentioned earlier the aspect of a "Magna Carta," I had in mind particularly the statement of public policy which is the introduction to the text of the statute.

Let us take note of its precise language from section 2 "1... the public policy of the United States is hereby declared as follows:

> Whereas under prevailing conditions developed with *the aid of governmental authority for owners of property to organize in the corporate and other forms of ownership association, the individual unorganized worker is commonly helpless to exercise actual liberty of contract and to protect his freedom of labor, and thereby to obtain acceptable terms and conditions of employment,* wherefore, though he should be free to decline to associate with his fellows, it is necessary that he have full freedom of association, self-organization, and designation of representatives of his own choosing, to negotiate the terms and conditions of his employment, and that he shall be free from the interference, restraint, or coercion of employers of labor, or their agents, in the designation

of such representatives or in self-organization or in other
concerted activities for the purpose of collective bargaining
or other mutual aid or protection; therefore the following
definitions of, and limitations upon, the jurisdiction and
authority of the courts of the United States are hereby
enacted. *(italics the author's)*

So far as my experience can determine this is the first general
commitment of the government to the cause of organized labor.
Note the mention of the right of owners of property to organize
in the corporate form, and how helpless are the individual unorganized workers.

If I had been a labor organizer these words would have appeared to me like a divine oracle. Although the Federal Courts
could not themselves establish organizations of labor, nevertheless, this statement represented the thinking of Congress, and it
was not difficult to see the logic of events that followed. I think
it is fair to recollect that the temper of Congress was influenced
by the plight of workers, everywhere, as a result of the Great
Depression, which in 1932 was revealing widespread distress and
unprecedented unemployment.

The year 1933 was the worst year of the Depression. Fifteen
million workers were unemployed, and those that had jobs were
likely to be on short time and on reduced pay. Wage and salary
cuts of those that had jobs were well nigh universal. Many normal
well educated persons who would rate as solid citizens were so
disturbed that many were saying that what the country needed
was a dictator. These people were serious. It is not my intention
here to describe the economic conditions of the 30's, except to
say the whole experience was a social and economic nightmare.
It came close to being a political nightmare.

The president asked for and received emergency powers from
the Congress. The National Industrial Recovery Act of 1933 authorized the President to establish Codes of Fair Competition
for each industry. These were made by Executive Order. Each

code had to include section 7 of the act which stipulated the following condition:

1. That employees shall have the right to organize and bargain collectively through representatives or in self-organization in other concerted activities for the purpose of collective bargaining or other mutual aid or protection.

2. That no employee and one seeking employment shall be required as a condition of employment to join any company union or to refrain from joining, organizing, or assisting a labor organization of his own choosing.

This section delighted the hearts of the labor organizers, but employers generally found the whole act very objectionable. Those employers who were not covered by a code were pressed to sign what was known as the President's Reemployment Agreement, which embodied the first paragraph quoted above.

So far as private industry was concerned there had been no government machinery to handle industrial disputes since the World War I Labor Board ended its function in 1919. Industry, was, in a sense, stunned. This was not war time; nevertheless, the circumstances of the Depression generated some unusual theories of government action. It must be remembered that these were the days of many new government functions which came to be identified by a long list of alphabetical agencies, such as PWA, NYA, WPA, HOLC, etc. [20]

There wasn't much business could do to resist government action. In proverbial language business was "flat on its back." If a business complied with the code, or with the President's re-employment agreement it could fly the "Blue Eagle." Not to fly the Blue Eagle, or to have the right to fly the Blue Eagle taken

---

[20] PWA–Public Works Administration; NYA–National Youth Administration; WPA–Works Progress Administration; HOLC–Home Owners Loan Corporation

away, was an invitation for public disfavor. Many union members interpreted the failure of the employer to fly the Blue Eagle as fair game for harassment, on the mistaken idea that now the employer had the government against him and was without his right of legal protection.

In Milwaukee, Wisconsin, the Electric and Transportation Utility did not sign the President's reemployment agreement. Some of the extreme unionists aided and abetted by communists had cells in several Milwaukee industries and perpetrated violence on the property of the utility until on one occasion a rioter stuck a pole through the fence of a transformer station and was electrocuted. After the strike was settled the company successfully sued the city for damages because of its failure to protect the utility property.

The Congress in the spring of 1934 passed a resolution known as Public Resolution No. 44. This authorized the President to establish a National Labor Relations Board to enforce the observance of the Section 7 A quoted above.

Soon after the passage of Resolution No. 44, there began a search for personnel to direct Regional Labor Boards. As a known student of labor economics, I was one of the nominees. Some of the directors chosen were political appointees. However, I myself was not a party worker for the New Deal, but I confess that like many others I had voted for the party in power. Having acquired a doctorate in Labor Economics some years prior, I was not without credentials for the appointment as Director of the Milwaukee Regional Labor Board. Of course my name had to be cleared with the chief Wisconsin labor leaders, and by a prominent Milwaukee industrialist who had previously cooperated with the New Deal administration in the enforcement of the N.R.A. Having passed that necessary obstacle, it was next necessary to obtain a leave of absence from Marquette University. The Dean in charge of my university responsibilities was ready to help me work out a plan to obtain a substitute for my classes, but it remained to obtain the consent of the President of the University. Fortunately, the Chairman of the National Labor Relations Board, Mr. Lloyd Garrison, came to Milwaukee to give an address on the union labor issues. I thought it available to induce him to see the President of the University to ask for my release. Before he left town the next morning, he paid a visit to the President's office. In a very short time, the die was cast, and I was soon subsequently formally appointed Associate Director of the Chicago Regional Labor Board.

The labor chiefs of Milwaukee were not altogether satisfied with that arrangement. They thought that the Milwaukee region was important enough to have its own regional board. Consequently, I became in fact Director of the Milwaukee Regional Labor Board. The Milwaukee Board was much less political than that of Chicago. My career training had been such as to condition me to perform a service as a public employee that would be fair to all interested parties. I tried to organize a board that would make a permanent contribution of fair dealing. I had the confidence of the local labor forces who backed my efforts. However, it is only fair to say that the employees of the N.L.R.B. in Washington did not appreciate my impartial administration. I was told, "This is a labor board for the benefit of organized labor." The inference was clear that the N.L.R.B. was not interested in impartial public services as I conceived it, but only in the degree that organized labor could be served. That was apparently the Board's conception of public service.

The local board was to consist of a panel of employers and labor representatives with a group of public members from whom would be selected a chairman for the respective tripartite panels chosen from the members of the board. These tripartite panels were to function in hearings of discrimination and other unfair labor practices of employers and to make decisions upon them. It was very difficult to obtain the services of employers. The President of the United States had made some very caustic charges against industrialists and businessmen. They had been called "economic royalists," "money changers," "malefactors of wealth," and the like. This, of course, did not make it easy for them to cooperate with the administration. I suspect that the work of assembling a local labor board did not go as fast as the members of the National Board thought it should. I was trying to build something substantial in the community. It could not be a "fly by night" organization, because being a well-known resident of this area I had to live with the results.

In due time we got matters rolling. However, emissaries from the national office urged that the work accomplished by the Board should be dramatized. Apparently the more spectacular the actions of the Board could be, the greater would be the appraisal of its success by the N.L.B. or the President. The pressure for speed was very great. According to some of the personnel of the National Board, the idea prevailed that issues should be dramatized and matters should be determined with greater acceleration. The attitude seemed to convey the idea that it should be understood that labor could not be wrong and that employers must consequently (because they are employers) seldom be right.[21]

Surely this was the overall psychology of the N.L.R.B. headquarters at the time. For an individual trained in the days of less pressing economic crises it was not a very comfortable situation. However, with the incorruptible leadership of Milwaukee labor, much permanent progress was made.

It must be realized that there had been for a long time a strong organized labor constituency of craft unions in Milwaukee in addition to the organization of unions in the brewing industry, to say nothing of the newspapers, railroads and the printing trades. Some of the spurious activity of organizations of "production"

---

[21] This was certainly true of the Executive Secretary and one member of the Board by the name of Edwin Smith.

workers was not enthusiastically appreciated by the established union forces.

The period of the N.I.R.A. lasted only a little more than a year, but there was much new organizing brought about in that time. There were issues arising in many quarters where employers had been, and still were, reluctant to accept unionization. Attempts were made to organize department stores, laundry workers, tannery employees, production workers in the steel and machinery works, structural iron workers, and the like. Some of these efforts were successful while others were not, but all of them presented problems to the Regional Board.

In order to understand the atmosphere – public and private – that pervaded the realm of labor relations under the New Deal, it may be of interest to give examples of the more significant experiences growing out of the exercise of public authority defending union organizations efforts. Section 7A of the National Industrial Recovery Act was designed to enable labor to organize and to exercise the right to bargain collectively with employers without interference. This clause made history. Organizers naturally took advantage of this new protection. Moreover they were encouraged by the Administration to organize. Labor organizers approaching individual workers would sell the union by insisting that the President of the United States wanted employees to join unions. This proved a vital incentive, and new unions sprang into being all around.

At this time, the efforts of the Communists temporarily aided and abetted the union movement in which they were fast infiltrating. To a trained economist who had specialized in the study of labor, this infiltration of Communists was very evident. Employers and the public were very gullible at first and did not understand that the activities of the new unions constituted a "front" for Communist activity. The union of tannery workers in Milwaukee was led by Communists, the union in the Seamon Body Corporation which made bodies for the Nash automobiles was for a time also dominated by Communists. Communists or their sympathizers were trouble-makers in the unions at this time even when they did not dominate them. It served no purpose to distinguish the tactics of Communists from those of legitimate trade unionists if people were not willing to believe, or if people did not understand that the goals were different. Communists wanted the unions to be tools for their political action. That is why they were most anxious to organize and dominate industrial unions. These types of unions were also favored by many employees of the N.L.R.B. To show the significance of this obsession, let me relate a revealing episode.

During the period of the administration of Section 7A by the first N.L.R.B. as the regional director, I received one morning a call from the Executive Secretary of the N.L.R.B. about a labor dispute which he said should have my immediate attention. I replied that I knew of the situation to which he referred, and that it was not as critical as the issue of an A.F. of L. dispute in the Paper Mill at Wisconsin Rapids. His reply was "Forget about the A.F. of L. In ten years there won't be any A.F. of L." The trade unionists wanted only economic action, that is, to achieve their goals through collective bargaining directly with the employer.

One of the first significant problems which I encountered as Director of Milwaukee Regional Labor Board in 1934 was a strike of Milwaukee laundry workers. This was an A.F. of L. union covering 25 laundries. Before I got on the scene, the meetings of the laundry owners and the union had broken up without any progress. It was incumbent on me to try and bring a settlement. I arranged for a meeting between the union and the representatives of the laundry owners. Section 7A of the N.R.A. states that the union could select representatives of its own choosing. The most militant members of this union had permitted the union to be represented by a "grandstand" exhibitionist who had come to Milwaukee from the East and who was endeavoring to "muscle in" on Milwaukee organized labor. A considerable group from the union was present at this meeting, serving as an audience for the grandiose play of this would-be labor leader. The first demand was for the "closed shop" (ie, all employees had to join the union, whether they wanted to or not). This brought immediate strong reaction from the employers and they promptly left the room. The attempted negotiations came to nothing. So the strike continued and the picket lines were operating in very inclement weather.

Since more of the pickets were women, I decided something must be done to end the strike even though there was no end in sight. I called on the president of the Milwaukee Central Labor Council for his aid in an effort to settle the strike. He was a very level-headed labor leader, and most cooperative. The National Union had given him authority to act for the local. We two arranged a meeting with the representative of the employers, a well-known Milwaukee lawyer. We got together in a hotel to see what could be done to reach a settlement. With the union demands in hand, I started out to discover, first of all, on what both parties could agree. As we went down the list we checked off all the items one by one except the matter of the closed shop. Each of us instinctively avoided the closed shop question. It proved to be a "straw man." On everything else we were agreed. Without anything more being said, we concluded that we had obtained an agreement. A meeting of the membership of the union was called and the proposed agreement was submitted for their ratification. They accepted it. At a subsequent meeting of the officers of the union and the laundry owners an agreement was signed.

There is a moral to this story. That is that satisfactory agreements are not made in group meetings which are led by demagogues. Representative democracy is more effective. The fiction of the "closed shop" was too strong a medicine for an industry which hitherto had been functioning without unions. Under the prevailing situation the laundry owners would never have consented to a closed shop. A closed shop is not essential to a work-able collective bargaining agreement.

Another experience worth relating was that concerning the strikes of 1934 in the Structural Steel Industry of Milwaukee. This strike had gone on for 13 weeks before I encountered it. Federal "conciliators" had made attempts to settle this strike to no avail. The individually owned company, whose 70-year old owner was opposed to the union and who threatened to close out the plant rather than sign a union agreement, was the hard-est "nut to crack." Now it was my responsibility to try and get an agreement. Being a local man, I knew of the idiosyncrasies of the owner, and consequently, I approached this company with some trepidation. I arranged to meet the works manager in his office. After I announced myself he told me that he had learned all about me – that I had resided in this community 24 years and was not a stranger to the nature of local conditions. He thought that in contrast to the conciliators from the U.S. Department of Labor who came from far away Washington D.C., he and I might be able to work out a solution. I did know what the anti-union employer complex in Milwaukee was. Therefore, the solution had to be tailored to the local conditions. The manager and I were able to communicate very well. We understood each other and there was mutual confidence. Confidence is the key word for satisfactory labor relations.

It was agreed between us that the manager and I could find a solution so that it would not be necessary to bother the owner with the problem. Fortunately, the owner acquiesced. The next step was to obtain the manager's story of his labor relations prob-lems, which he gave me in full detail. His story sounded convinc-ing. I asked him if he would be willing to tell the same story to the union representatives in my presence. He assured me he was.

I next obtained the story from the spokesman of the union to the same effect. Would they be willing to repeat their story to the plant manager in my presence? They in turn promised that they would. Later, we held a joint session where each party presented its story to the other. I then turned to the manager and said, "You have worked with these men for 25 years. Do you believe that they are telling you the truth?"

"Yes," said the manager, "I know these men and I know they would not lie."

Then I said to the union men, "You have known your boss for 25 years. Do you believe that he is telling a straight story?" They were strong on their affirmation that they had every confidence in the manager and had great respect for him. They were all men of good will. There was mutual confidence. It remained now to find the technical solution.

A few observations are necessary here before concluding this story. Milwaukee had been and still was a center of anti-union propaganda for the "open shop," called the "American Plan" carried on with great vigor in the 20's and dying hard in the 30's. The employers had hired a journalist to write defensive literature for them, and to play down the value of unions, and particularly the closed shop, or what now is termed the "Union Shop." These employers were more or less honor-bound to close ranks against the union, therefore, they shied away from any written agreement for fear of disdain from their fellow employers. How was one to break through this barrier?

In the situation under discussion the employer expressed his belief that terms could be arrived at if the outside union organizer was left out of the picture. I approached the union International Vice President, who was the outsider who knew the facts of the situation, and he agreed to stay out of the negotiations, if the company kept their propaganda journalist out of the situation. This was mutually agreed. Now it was necessary to pave the way for an agreement.

The manager now was willing after hearing the union's complaints to grant the wishes of the union, but could not under the prevailing conditions express everything in writing. He made certain limited concessions on paper, but promised verbally he would do more than the agreement indicated. If the men would believe him they could get what they wanted without embarrassment to the owner and therefore save both the firm and their jobs. They did believe him. They had confidence in his word. The union approved the terms. Good labor relations at this point established in 1934 have continued into the 1960's without interruption. Each party had confidence in the integrity of the other, and a desire for fair play.

I would now like to relate an experience to show what lack of confidence can do. One morning in the beginning of winter an officer of the Milwaukee Central Trades and Labor Council came to my office to see if I could help in a dispute in a firm where the employees threatened a strike of 700 workers. The employees of the firm were determined to walk out. The union leader referred to knew that this would be disastrous to the firm which at the time was losing money, and also to the permanent jobs of the workers, since a strike would mean a permanent loss of orders essential to this enterprise. This union business agent, in the best interest of the workers, tried to convince these workers not to strike.

However, the men did not have confidence in their leader. The reason seemed to be that when the business agent went to the plant in a new Chevrolet which, of course, was parked outside of the plant, the men proclaimed, contrary to fact, that this had been bought for him by the management of the firm; hence, the union had been "sold out."

It was suggested that perhaps I, as the Labor Board Director, could meet with the men to dissuade them from striking. I agreed to try my hand. When I arrived at the plant, about 20 principals of the union membership assembled in a large office space where the books of the company were spread out on a large table. I inquired about the union complaints. The men said they wanted a raise in wages. However, company books showed the concern had been operating in the red for the four months past. The owner of the business had promised to give the men an increase in wages as soon as the business could operate in the black. I asked the men how they could expect to get an increase under the conditions, since one could not get blood out of a turnip. Why would they not accept the owner's offer of an increase as soon as he was out of the red? They responded that these were a false set of books, although in fact they were audited by Price and Waterhouse and were the authentic records accepted by the Federal Internal Revenue Department.

Arriving at this stalemate, I then asked the workers what else they wanted, besides an increase in wages. They said that they wanted a "contract." In other words, they wanted a collective bargaining agreement. After a slight hesitation, I expressed profound shock. What fools they must be! They wanted a written agreement from a man they accused of being a "crook." Only fools made arrangements with crooks. What good was an agreement with a person whose word was not honored? They had accused their boss of dishonesty with the books. How could they expect that his written word would be any better? An agreement is no better than the person who makes it! The men began to see the ridiculous situation in which they had placed themselves. After this demonstration of stupidity, the President of the Milwaukee Central Labor Council who accompanied me at the time, suggested that the leaders of the union meet with him in his office the following day. This they did, and a satisfactory accommodation was soon effected.

Labor relations is a phase of human behavior with many facets. If it were possible to know what is in the other fellow's mind in these disputes, the solutions would obviously come more easily. To illustrate with a case in point: A manufacturing concern with 1200 workers in a northern Michigan town had a dispute which threatened economic disaster for the city for a good part of the winter, including the Christmas season. I had been asked by a high ranking Milwaukee labor leader to see if I could not help in this solution so as to preclude the walk-out which the union had voted to undertake. In response to his request, I spent one day with the union representatives and another day with the management. I could see no reason for a strike. There seemed to be no real cleavage between the parties that one could see. With the approval of the union, I arranged for a joint session in the offices of the company to consider the terms of the proposed agreement. As we discussed the individual stipulations of the union's demands, it was apparent that there was mutual agreement. Still the manager of the corporation would not sign.

What could be the reason? After a private talk with the manager, he confided that he would not sign a joint document with the union although he agreed to all the conditions of employment put forth by the union. I asked "Why?" He then told me that he had been instructed by the vice-president of the company who lived in the East that he should by no means put his name on the same paper with that of the union. He said the unions could hold the employer to an agreement, but the employer could not bind a union.

That was the real issue in this dispute. How was the union to meet this issue if it did not know that it existed? This was before the Wagner Act, which required a bona-fide contract in writing. All that the law required at this time was an "agreement." This solution was satisfactorily concluded through our regional labor board office by the following procedure. The employer was to send to my office the stipulations upon which he agreed to hire the members of the union. I was to forward this document to the union and have its members certify that they agreed to accept these stipulations. Peace was maintained. This may not have been a "contract." However, the parties had certainly come to an agreement concerning wages, hours, and working conditions.

Very often the root reason for a labor dispute is not on the surface. It is very frequently caused by a lack of communication.

There is another consideration which seems to me to be worthy of mention. Forcing sudden changes in human relations by statute is bound to carry some negative factors. When one reflects on the impact of the New Deal philosophy on the part of employers of labors, it appears as though the government by fiat was trying to effect a reform in labor relations which normally requires a generation.

Human behavior is not easily changed. To obtain general acceptance of a new way of life, a transition period of conditioning is essential. Naturally, when the N.R.A. enforcement upset so drastically the long accepted pattern of industrial relations which had been established in custom and law, it was not to be expected that employers would embrace the "New Deal religion" without resistance. It must be remembered that the N.L.R.B. in enforcing Section 7A of the Industrial Recovery Act was engaged in a history making endeavor. It was no less significant than sounding the death-knell of "laissez-faire." Since individualism had been a concomitant of the Industrial Revolution and the hand-maid of American prosperity, it is not difficult to understand why many employers resisted. The sudden shifts in the behavior norms of industrial relations were bound to bring mutual friction and distrust with its by-product of violence.

One disconcerting aspect of the enforcement of N.R.A. was the vindictiveness of some of the personnel of the N.L.R.B. It seemed at least to one member of the board of three that nothing was so sweet as an opportunity to make employees squirm.

As a functionary of the local board, I was embarrassed by directions from Washington telling me what action I must take toward the employer. To give a case in point: A discrimination charge was brought against a Milwaukee concern which came to a hearing before members of the local board. The hearing brought out overwhelming evidence to sustain the employer's contention of innocence of the charge. The case was appealed to the National Labor Relations Board which sustained the findings of the local board. However, the decision did not rest on its merits, for although the case of discrimination was resolved without prejudice to the employer, a member of the N.L.R.B. went out of his way to criticize some other actions of the employer, which resulted in instructions to me to go to the factory of this employer to see, myself, that a specific notice which was dictated to me, was placed on the factory bulletin board. The notice was to the effect that "the employer has been a bad boy, was now penitent, and would promise to be good in the future." This was a very distasteful experience for me, since I knew the employer quite well, who was really trying his best to cooperate with the Washington powers.

On May 27, 1935, the United States Supreme Court declared the N.L.R.A. unconstitutional.[22] The Court held that legislative powers had been given to the President by the Congress which Congress did not have the right to confer on the Chief Executive.

Although the New Deal proponents at the time took the invalidation of the N.R.A. as a calamity, it seemed to me a very fortunate circumstance that the U.S. Supreme Court recognized the N.R.A.'s departure from the principles of the Constitution. In my academic pursuits at the time, a colleague placed in my hands a copy of the constitution of Mussolini's Fascist State. It was astonishing to see how in many ways the establishment of Industry codes by Executive Order paralleled the functioning of the National Guilds of the Italian Fascist State.

The demise of the N.R.A. was not a calamity as subsequent experience showed, for within a month Congress passed another Statute which incorporated the famous Section 7A of the In-

---

[22] Schechter Poultry Co. vs. U.S. (1935 295. U.S. 495)

dustry Recovery Act, and set up an agency to avoid unfair labor practices on the part of the employers of laborers so that labor could organize unions without interference. Under this statute organized labor prospered mightily. This act, officially known as the National Labor Relations Act, was introduced by New York Senator Robert Wagner, and became law July 5, 1935. This was another landmark in the history of labor relations. Here was a bid to establish the Federal Government as a protector and promoter of organized labor and of collective bargaining.

Since these pages have been centered around the activities of public authorities and labor relations, I would like to draw attention to the declaration of policy contained in the Wagner Act of July 5, 1935.

The full statement has five paragraphs comprising over 500 words. It gives a complete rationalization for the act depicting the intent of the Congress so that the Courts would be in no doubt as to what was in the minds of the lawmakers. However, the second section of this statement revealed the philosophy of the New Deal proponents of this statute. The section reads:

> The inequality of bargaining power between employees who do not possess full freedom of association or actual liberty of contract, and employers who are organized in the corporate or other forms of ownership association substantially burdens and affects the flow of commerce and tends to *aggravate recurrent business depressions, by depressing wage rates and the purchasing power of wage earners in industry,* and by preventing the stabilization of competitive wage rates and working conditions within and between industries. *(Italics, author's)*

The above paragraph represents the philosophy of the New Deal "advisors" and seems to me to have great validity. The next section, however, suggests the rationalization of the politicians, and embodies wishful thinking. It reads:

> Experience has proved that protection by law of the
> right of employees to organize and bargain collectively
> safeguards commerce from injury, impairment or
> interruption and promotes the flow of commerce by
> removing certain recognized sources of industrial strife
> and unrest, by encouraging practices fundamental to the
> friendly adjustment of industrial disputes arising out of
> differences as to wages, hours, or other working conditions,
> and by restoring equality of bargaining power between
> employers and employees.

The experience in the protection by law mentioned in the above statement could only mean the protection of employees under the Railway Labor Act. There was no such experience in private industry, and furthermore private industry up to this time was not considered to be in interstate commerce and therefore not under federal authority. The framers of the law were counting on a similar labor relations experience in private industry as that which had prevailed on the Railways under the Railway Labor Act of 1926.

If labor in private industry had shown more restraint, the results might more nearly have been characterized by the pronouncements of the law makers. It would be contrary to fact to claim that under the Wagner Act there was less interference with commerce than before.

The fifth and final paragraph of this lengthy statement of public policy contains the following:

> It is hereby declared to be the policy of the United States
> to eliminate the causes of certain substantial obstructions
> to the free flow of commerce and to mitigate and eliminate
> these obstructions when they have occurred by *encouraging
> the practice and procedure of collective bargaining* and by
> protecting the exercise by the workers of the full freedom
> *of their employment of other mutual aid or protection. (Italics,
> author's)*

The installment process of gains seemed to have been forgotten. Many times the unions set their stakes high – "all or nothing." This experience under the Wagner Act gave the country 12 years of industrial turmoil.

The lesson of the Wagner Act so far as labor is concerned is as old as civilization. Freedom must be accompanied by restraint. The new power conferred on labor by the decision of the Supreme Court in the Jones & Loughlin case extending the concept of interstate commerce to cover labor relations in private industry, was pushed to excess. The strikes in the steel, coal, automobile and shipping industries showed that the unions were pushing their weight around and bargaining goals were attained by force or attrition. The old technique of the craft unions—improvements were obtained on a piece meal basis—was ignored.

As might be expected, this tonic to organized labor found a popular response. We were still not out of the Depression. The philosophy of the New Deal permeated the public authorities of many industrial states of the union. Within two years after the passage of the Wagner Act, a number of states enacted laws patterned after the Wagner Act and were referred to as "Baby Wagner Acts." One noteworthy example was that of my own state of Wisconsin. The same phenomenon of labor's abuse of its power on a federal basis became a characteristic on the state level. When the Wisconsin law was being framed, some more conservative friends of labor urged the passage of a law that would not be one-sided but be a fair law under which both management and labor could prosper. This proposal was made to the chief spokesman for the labor forces. However, the response came in the words, "This is going to be a labor law for the benefit of labor. We have sufficient friends in the legislature to pass such a law, and we are going to have it." It was unfortunate that the state labor leaders did not improve on the Wagner Act, for the consequences were quite disillusioning for those who believed in fair play for both sides.

It must be recalled that this act, like the National Labor Relations Act, outlawed a series of what were conceived to be unfair practices of employers, but put no restraints on the action of unions. The assumption, therefore, was to the effect that organized labor and its leaders did not engage in unfair labor practices. This assumption, naturally, soon proved to be erroneous. Within two years, Wisconsin employers, including farmers cooperatives, producers of perishable commodities, and distributors of dairy products found the activities of the unions so harassing and financially embarrassing that they clamored for a new labor relations statute. They combined their forces and hired a reputable and able lawyer to produce the draft of a new statute to replace the baby Wagner Act. This attorney took wide counsel among students of labor and other experienced specialists in the field of labor relations, and prepared a bill to be submitted to the Wisconsin Legislature of 1939. The political complex of the legislature was favorable for the repeal of the act of 1937. The new proposal was enacted into law in 1939, and became known as the Wisconsin Employment Peace Act. This act was a pioneer piece of legislation. It contained some significant provisions not to be found hitherto in any labor relations statute.

Of great importance is the public policy statement of this act, expressed by the following statement.

> It (the State) recognizes that there are three major interests
> involved namely: That of the public, the employee, and
> the employer. These three interests are to a considerable
> extend interrelated. It is the policy of the state to protect
> and promote each of these interests with due regard to the
> situation and to the rights of others.[23]

The above statement is a tacit recognition that labor disputes

---

[23] Statutes of Wisconsin, Chap. III - (1).

are not matters pertaining only to unions and management, but involve the direct and indirect interests of the public who ostensibly constitute a third party in every dispute, even though it may be a silent partner.

While the fact of public interest in labor disputes was not a new discovery, it was something new to have this fact acknowledged by explicit language in a labor relations statute.

There is a second aspect of this Wisconsin Employment Peace Act which shows its pioneer character, and that is the fact that this statute not only outlawed unfair labor practices on the part of the employer but proscribed unfair practices of the unions as well. This was a departure from the practice of the Wagner Act which gave no mention of union unfair labor practices, as I have indicated earlier.

The Wisconsin Employment Peace Act is a more realistic labor relation act than any that had preceded it, and incidentally has operated satisfactorily to all parties, so far as its jurisdiction, curtailed by Federal usurpation, extends.

The significant contribution of this Wisconsin statute was to point the direction in which the Federal Labor Relations legislation should take. The outstanding features of the Wisconsin statute were in principle written into the Federal law in the year 1947.

During the twelve years following the enactment of the Wagner Act, the labor unions made substantial growth in numbers and power, both economic and political. Congressional inquiry into the conduct of labor relations prior to 1947 revealed the need for the imposition of legal restraints upon unions and their leaders in order to protect the public interest. Not only is the employer affected by the malfunction of union power, but more and more pointedly the public is inconvenienced and frequently shocked. The findings of the Congressional inquiry resulted in the passage of the Taft Hartley Act of 1947. This act has its history-making facets. It followed the Wisconsin example of proscribing unfair labor practices of unions as well as those of employers. It also reflected changing public policy by recognizing as Wisconsin had done that the public is a silent partner in all industrial disputes. Note what is mentioned in the public statement of the act. Among other things it states:

> Industrial strife which interferes with the normal flow of commerce and with the full production of articles and commodities for commerce, can be avoided or substantially minimized if employers, employees, and labor organizations each recognize under law one another's legitimate rights and obligations in their relations with each other, and above all recognize under law that neither party has any right in its relations with any other to engage in acts or practices which jeopardize the *public health, safety, or interest.* [24]

This act required unions to bargain in good faith where the Wagner Act had prescribed bargaining in good faith only for employers. Furthermore, a significant feature of this statute was to set up an independent government Mediation Service divorced entirely from the Department of Labor. This was designed to win the confidence of employers who had felt that the old Conciliation Service in the Department of Labor was partial to labor.

This is not an attempt to analyze the Taft Hartley Act, but to show how public policy toward labor disputes was changing, and to indicate that public opinion was demanding that organized labor should be held responsible as are other institutions in our society.

The reaction of labor leaders to this law was violent. The cohorts of labor were flooded with propaganda attempting to force repeal of the law. It was dubbed a "slave labor law," "a bonanza for lawyers," etc., etc. For several years the campaign for repeal was

---

[24] Prentice-Hall Labor Course, p. 30, 401. Italics, Author's.

a big crusade of labor. However, the strikes in the coal, steel, and auto industries carried on with little regard for the interests of the public, and with little restraint, made it impossible for public opinion to sanction a continuation of the experiences encountered under the Wagner Act.

A few weeks after the Taft Hartley Act was passed, I was invited to discuss and explain this act to groups of union men in a Wisconsin city. I pointed out its constructive features and how bona fide union men would be benefitted by the act.

My efforts were not well received. One of my university students who hailed from that city informed me that I had better not show up there again. My name was, consequently, in disrepute. The response to this act on the part of organized labor was an emotional one. It really did place some limitations on the actions of union leaders but it in no way curtailed or obligated any legitimate interest or rights of union men. The younger generation of students of labor, who had obtained a smattering of labor experience during the period of World War II, seemed to join the parade of critics who falsely claimed that the law was anti-union and should be repealed. There were also others among labor economists who failed to take an objective view of the merits of the law.

Attempts were made in Congress to repeal this law, but to no avail. The Congressmen who knew the sentiments of their constituents did not dare to flaunt public opinion by repealing the law.

Senator Bob Taft of Ohio, one of the authors of the law came up for election in 1950. The organized labor forces of the state, with the aid of the Democratic Party turned on all their guns, and spent large sums of money to defeat the senator, as a presumed enemy of labor.

Mr. Taft campaigned at the factory gates defending the Taft Hartley Act, explaining it in detail. He was overwhelmingly reelected. The significant thing about this election was the fact that

Republican Senator Taft received a plurality of 500,000 votes in the same election that Frank G. Lausche, the Democratic candidate for Governor of Ohio won a plurality of 400,000.

This circumstance put the quietus on the campaign to repeal the Taft Hartley Act.

It must be pointed out that although many people speak of this statute as being one to effect a balance of bargaining power by giving a better break for the employer, that this is not a proper appraisal of the reason for its enactment. The prime motive of the Congress was definitely to protect the *public* interest. It is on this issue that the law should be appraised.

While not affecting collective bargaining directly, a subsequent statute bearing on labor relations was the "Labor-Management Reporting and Disclosure Act of 1959."

The newly acquired power of organized labor to bargain for pensions and welfare funds following Taft Hartley created other problems of great social import. Huge sums of money built up under employee welfare and security provisions of collective bargaining contracts afforded many opportunities for irregularities in the handling of union funds, particularly in the newer types of unions. The temptation to manipulate union elections is a strong drug for the labor racketeers when so large amounts of money are involved.

In Congress in 1957 the McClellan Committee on Improper Activities in Labor and Management revealed the corruption of certain unions and the deprivation of the rights of individual union members and other related abuses. These caused a public revulsion which led to the enactment of another labor relation statute known as the Labor Management Reporting and Disclosure Act of 1959.

Again it is fitting to examine the public policy statement of the act. Section 2(b) contains the following significant language:

The Congress further finds, from recent investigations

in the labor and management fields that there have been
a number of instances of breach of trust, corruption,
disregard of the rights of individual employees, and other
failures to observe high standards of responsibility and
ethical conduct which require further and supplementary
legislation that will afford necessary protection of the
rights and interests of employees and the public generally
as they relate to the activities of labor organizations,
employers, labor relations consultants, and their officers
and representatives.

(c) The Congress, therefore, further finds and declares
that the enactment of this act is necessary to eliminate
or prevent improper practices on the part of labor
organization, employers, labor relations consultants and
their officers and representatives which distort and defeat
the policies of the Labor Management Relations Act, 1947
. . . .

In summary this act under Title I establishes a bill of rights
of members of labor organizations. Title II requires reporting by
labor organizations officers and employees of labor organizations
and employers. Title III establishes the proper conduct and responsibilities of union trusteeships. Title IV provides terms and
procedures for the election of union officers. Title V requires fi-
duciary responsibility of officers of labor organizations. Title VI
provides for investigation, makes unlawful extortionate picketing, clarifies relation to other statutes and establishes administrative procedure. Title VII deals with amendments to the Labor
Management Relations Act of 1947.

These provisions are important since in effect they "plug up"
the loopholes which had become apparent with the enforcement
of the Labor Management Relations Act. They are of significant
importance and can be summarized as follows:

1   The question of Federal-State jurisdiction was resolved to

eliminate the "no man's land" where for technical reasons the Federal government did not assume jurisdiction, and the state did not have authority to do so.

2. The National Labor Relations Board was given the right to delegate its authority.

3. Economic strikers are permitted to vote in representative elections.

4. Secondary boycotts are proscribed.

5. Hot cargo agreements are prohibited.

6. Statutory restrictions are placed on recognition and organizational types of picketing.

The net result of these amendments is to improve the administration of the labor relations statutes and to effect more consistently the public policy set forth by the lawmakers when enacting the statutes under review.

In bringing to a close this analysis of the labor relations legislative framework, it is important to note that 25 states have passed Anti-Injunction laws, and about a score of states have enacted Right to Work laws. Right to work laws guarantee the right of workers to hold a job without the necessity of joining a union. In other words they outlaw the "all union shop." However, in a recent Indiana case the Supreme Court has held valid what is called the Agency Shop. This permits the union to assess fees on non-union workers for services rendered when they work in shops where terms and conditions of employment are determined by union collective bargaining agreements.

How these various statutes affect the contending parties in particular situations must be left to the lawyers. The attempt in this paper has been to present the general framework of legislation which conditions the collective bargaining procedures. It points up to the fact that when the contending parties exercise a lack of restraint and mutual regard for each other's rights and that of the public, the heavy hand of the law must take over to set the limits and bounds of economic and social behavior characteristic of modern industrial conflict. Only thus can a free society be maintained.

Of course it is regrettable that the thousands of good unions which have operated on the "up and up" have to be saddled with the burden of complicated reporting because of the few that created a public menace. However, in our highly integrated industrial society this phenomenon seems to be a necessary concomitant. It still remains a truism that effective collective bargaining cannot be legislated but must be the result of mutual understanding and cooperation for the common good.

Chapter VIII

SOME CAREER HIGHLIGHTS

Whatsoever a man soweth that shall they also reap.
—St. Paul

One often hears the question, "How did you get started in your career?" The answer usually given conveys the idea that circumstances and accident had a bearing on the final direction in which one pursues a career. Of course, it is true that a person who takes graduate work usually finds that he has an opportunity to move in one of several directions as a result of his advanced study, that is, in his field of interest.

In another connection, I have already related my experience concerning the civil service assignment as State Supervisor of Apprenticeship. To administer a new statute on apprentices and be the first state supervisor of apprenticeship in modern times, if not the first state supervisor of apprenticeship in history, was a thrilling challenge. There was one thing certain, that if I could not devise what should be done to administer the law, there was no one who could tell me. The whole process had to be thought out very thoroughly, working principles had to be established and rules and regulations set up. I was not a genuine "bureaucrat," and I determined to be a good one. It was not long before Wisconsin made history with its new apprenticeship law and attracted the attention of other states and countries all over the world.

The opportunity for interesting contacts in the areas of industry, education and government administration was very great. This position of responsibility, unique in character, was certainly one of the first highlights of my career. Furthermore it reinforced my conviction that if an individual does well in the job in hand, he is certain to be considered capable of doing well in another responsibility. So it proved with me.

The administration of the apprenticeship law necessitated an advisory committee known as the State Committee on Apprenticeship, which had representation from industry and labor. The manufacturer, who was the chairman of this committee and who had observed my work over a number of years, was desirous of having my services for his concern. This was the year 1920, soon after World War I, when it was beginning to be appreciated that in order for an employer to handle labor and employee situations adequately it was necessary to have an organized personnel department with a functionary—a Personnel Manager or a Director of Industrial Relations—qualified to meet the necessities of such a program.[25]

Mr. E. J. Kearney, who was the chairman and president of the Kearney-Trecker Manufacturing Company, asked me one day if I would meet him at the bank of which he was also president. I met him there and we sat side by side on a bench with his partner, Theodore Trecker, who sat on the other side of me. They both engaged in an animated conversation to convince me that I should resign my position with the State of Wisconsin and take an assignment with their corporation. This posed a very serious question. Should I leave public employment for private industry? In many respects my job as State Supervisor of Apprenticeships seemed to have definite limitations. To put it another way, the job itself did not offer sufficient scope for the abilities I had cultivated.

---

[25] See Chapter VI.

Strangely enough, I had many times said to myself and to my friends that I would never work for a business corporation. However, I talked the thing out and resolved that the experience would be something which would help to qualify me for further opportunities and that I might incidentally make some contribution to the cause of employer - employee relations. Finally I accepted the position and became Director of Personnel at this company on April 1st, 1920.

The experience seemed very rewarding for a period of a few months. However, by the middle of 1920 a post-war depression set in. This necessitated the laying off of many employees and again reducing the scope of activities for the situation I was in. It gave me great insight to some of the malpractices of industry at that particular time.

One day late in the fall of that year, Mr. Theodore Trecker, the partner in this enterprise, attended a meeting in the city of Milwaukee which was addressed by Roger Babson. Mr. Babson was an economist well known as a forecaster. He told these men assembled in this meeting that the economic situation was grave and that it was necessary that business should conserve and be cognizant of the consequences of the declining prosperity. As a result, Mr. Trecker came back to the plant and immediately made contact with the employment manager and told him to lay off forty people and not to let any grass grow under his feet while doing it.

This really was not the whim of a hard employer which Mr. Trecker might appear to be. It was a practice characteristic of the times. This came as a shock to me, because every one of the forty people involved had worked with this company for at least a period of ten years. They were to get the first lay-off in their experience, to take place the same afternoon as they received what is known as the "pink slip."

I thought this procedure, although prevalent at the time, to be rather inhuman. It seemed to me the individuals involved should have had a little time or some cushion to receive the shock of the layoff, since one can't tell what the condition of the worker's home might be. I thought it incumbent upon the firm to give these individuals some notice, and that the layoff could take effect at some later date.

I remember that at a meeting of the Industrial Relations Association of Wisconsin held in Madison, at a subsequent date, I raised strong objection to such a practice. I convinced some of the manufacturers that there ought to be a better method of accomplishing layoffs than was the practice at the time. Let it be said that in subsequent years, improvements were made in methods of reducing the payroll. It should be pointed out that this was years before the "New Deal," and the impact of organized labor.

To illustrate the strange psychology of many employers at the time, I can relate a story that I know of an employer who notified his office staff that their salary would be cut 20% and that this would take effect retroactively. In other words, after the people had probably committed their salaries, they would discover that their next pay checks were not to be what they expected. This mistake of making the salary retroactive was compounded by a request on the part of this employer to his office staff on the same day, to have them go into the company garage, at the first opportunity, to see his new Cadillac.[26] While, of course, there was no connection, nevertheless, many of the employees would get the idea that their cut in salary was what helped to pay for the new Cadillac. At any event the psychology of the incident was tragic.

In 1920 the personnel management movement, going strong at the time, (although still in its early stages), was promoted to

---

[26] When I told this to my students, I heard one of them say to another, referring to me, "Did you ever hear such a liar?" It seemed impossible to believe. However, it was the ungarnished truth.

avoid such practices and to develop a better relationship between employers and their workers. Unions were scarcely in the picture in manufacturing industries during this period. I realized in a relatively short time that I could not devote my full energies indefinitely to the situation as it then existed. I was, however, offered a job with a large company in the East with six plants to function as Personnel Director. However, I did not accept because I knew that the manufacturers of that particular period were, in the main, using personnel departments and techniques with the object of avoiding the prospect of unions in their plants. After being a student of labor economics, I could not give myself to the task of working with the view of defeating the legitimate aspirations of labor.

By the first of the year 1922, I was requested by the Director of Rehabilitation for the state of Wisconsin to make a survey in Milwaukee industries to discover what opportunities there were for handicapped workers. I took on this assignment which covered a period of five months. However, I was not released from my position with the Kearney and Trecker Corp. but was held on a retainer, which incidentally I held for another eight years on a part-time basis.

Upon completion of the assignment for the State Rehabilitation authorities, I determined on a plan to visit Europe and the family in England. I had not seen my mother for 14 years. In the meantime, however, I was approached by authorities at Marquette University to take a position with them as the Coordinator of the Cooperative Engineering Program. The university spokesman was interested in obtaining my experience on apprenticeship which could ostensibly be applied to the apprenticeship of Marquette engineering students in industry. Furthermore, I was acquainted with the industrial clientele, so to speak, because of my years with the Industrial Commission and my connections in association with Milwaukee industries.

Before I went to Europe, I had committed myself to accept

the position with Marquette University as a Professor of Economics and Industrial Relations in charge of the co-operative engineers program and to teach economics to engineering students. This appointment was to take effect on September 1st, 1922. [27]

When the president of the Kearney & Trecker Company learned of my planned visit abroad, he suggested that I should plan, as a good will gesture, to call on the European exporters, who had business relations with the Milwaukee concern. Consequently, on this overseas trip I visited Burton & Griffiths in London, Stokvis & Sons in Paris and in Brussels, also an exporting house in Rotterdam, and a branch concern in Berlin. I found out in Berlin why it was difficult to sell Milwaukee milling machines to the Germans. It appears the Germans had copied the machines and were making it themselves by exploiting the U.S. registered patents.

One of the things that impressed me about this visit was the character of the furnishings in the offices of these export houses. I made an observation to Mr. Stokvis in Brussels, that the office furniture and equipment contrasted greatly with the more or less plain utilitarian furnishings of the American business offices. I had to express my admiration and in reply he said to me, "I spend one-third of my life in this place. Why should I not have a situation which is pleasing and comfortable?" I thought he had the right philosophy.

In subsequent years, I have noticed great changes in American offices, and now perhaps our office furnishings many times are as elaborate and artistic as the European, although we don't see oriental rugs very often in American offices.

In thinking about aesthetics, I was conscious in 1922 that it was strikingly apparent that we in the United States were far behind the Europeans in appreciation and execution of art. The less angular street intersections of European cities such as Lon-

---

[27] See Chap V, p. 85.

don, Paris, Brussels, and Berlin had a pleasing effect. In comparison, American cities with the boxlike street intersections seem to be crude. Moreover, our telephone and electric wire support poles with rectangular cross arms, contrasted unfavorably with the graceful top installations of the French, for example, where poles and wire installations were mounted with pleasing curves. This was in 1922 and also in 1937. However, today in the 1960s it is not so true.

In these intervening years in thousands of ways in the evolution of industrial art, pleasing architectural design, and general aesthetic appreciation, the development of the U.S. has been quite astounding. One of the most significant aspects of the development of our culture during the past half century, in my opinion based on interested observations, is the development of all forms of art and artistic expression in the United States. The development of our industrial art has been especially impressive.

This European trip was soon after World War I. It was appalling to read the long list of war casualties posted in all the many cities and villages that I saw. The United States' effort in World War I was not then very highly evaluated or appreciated. We entered the war after the Allies were exhausted, and secured the victory. Our Allies seemed to resent the expression on the part of Americans, "We won the war." This attitude, however, was to change by 1926 on my second trip to which I shall later refer. It looked very much as though the country of England was being Americanized. Our movies for better or for worse were changing the pattern of thought. The advertising of American products abounded everywhere, although there were slogans, widespread, exhorting people to buy British products. I noticed that the display of typewriters which were shown as British products included the Remington, Underwood, and some other well known American makes. This, of course, was evidence that United States manufacturers had branch facilities in other countries and particularly in Britain.

In 1922 the radio was in its infancy, and in spite of the war, ordinary people were not internationally sophisticated.

On the eastward passage of the Atlantic liner most of the passengers were tourists bound for the battlefields of France. Many were war widows. The dance and musical theme of the relatively young passengers of the ship was all pervading and incessant. It seemed that all the way of the journey the strains were repeated, "I want to be happy, but I can't be happy, 'til I make you happy, too" (the by-product of a 1916 Ziegfield Follies show, which incidentally my wife and I saw in Philadelphia while on our honeymoon).

On the return trip a phenomenon I cannot forget was the many passengers of young Irishmen in priestly garb, who certainly were not priests, but rather Sinn Feiners, no doubt of the Irish Rebellion, escaping the British authorities by emigrating to the New World.

September 1, 1922, I began my career at Marquette University as Coordinator for Engineering Co-op students and as Professor of Economics. This subject of economics was a new addition to the engineering curriculum and it was assumed by many to be a subject foreign to engineering students and apparently heartily disliked by them. This I found to be untrue. It was entirely a matter of presentation and of enlistment of the student's interest from his point of view. The function of an engineer in our economy is manifestly so vital that it is difficult to imagine how the students could avoid the study of economics without limiting their professional possibilities and outlook. I really enjoyed teaching economics to the student engineers. They were a stimulating group.

The co-operative engineering program has many things to recommend it in a dynamic industrial complex. The considerations which apply to trade apprenticeship also apply here. While the student is pursuing his academic training, he is also being put through the crucible of experience in the world of practical realities.

While carrying on this arrangement, I still functioned as Director of Industrial Relations of the Kearney and Trecker Corporation on a part-time basis, involving two afternoons each week. My acquaintance with industry was now unique, a fact which contributed greatly to the service I could render to Marquette University and its engineering students.

Prosperity was now on the increase. World War I had accelerated technological advance which was to be accentuated during the following years until upset by the Great Depression of the thirties. During these years of prosperity following World War I, there was a quickened pace in American life. Interest in scientific management became almost universal. As a derivative, the science and art of personnel management was being emphasized. More and more companies were establishing personnel departments to carry on welfare programs. Improvement of employee selection, placement, and training had a strong emphasis in all these programs.

However, it must be said that improvement in industrial relations in the twenties was motivated, in the main, to avoid the spread of union organization among the employees which employers regarded as an anathema. To aid and abet this effort to block unionism, there was launched the "Open Shop" movement. This was a particular objective of the National Metal Trades Association and the National Association of Manufacturers. It was not really a movement for the open shop but in reality was an anti-union shop movement. In the long run this was bound to fail. It was not a movement which contributed to a more equitable distribution of the national income. The collapse of the economy at the end of the decade seemed to doom the future of the open shop or the American Plan as it was called.

In the early twenties, as indicated elsewhere, vocational education was developing rapidly. Some bottlenecks, so to speak, were painfully apparent to those of us placing young people in industrial employment. One of those bottlenecks was the lack of vocational guidance. It very often occurs that significant impetus for improvement does not always come from the professionals themselves, but is often pressed into focus by outsiders in the area which receives the product of the professionals.

Due to the persistence of one Marjorie Gillette, at the time in charge of personnel of the Robert A. Johnson Company of Milwaukee, a number of business and industrial personnel directors gathered together to promote vocational guidance departments in the Milwaukee high schools and in the Milwaukee vocational schools. Our efforts succeeded. The Milwaukee School Board established a guidance department in the high schools and so did the Milwaukee Vocational School, subsequent to our recommendation.

Some of these previously mentioned group of personnel directors made another significant contribution to the Milwaukee community. Although at the time it seemed only to be a "run of the mill" matter, the story is worth telling. Dr. Arthur Rowland, a former Dean of Drexel Institute of Philadelphia, at this time Educational Director of the Milwaukee Electric, Railway and Light Company; Mr. Horace Frommelt, Personnel Manager of the Falk Corporation; Mr. Van Cleaf of the Allis-Chalmers Manufacturing Company; and I, after discussing the subject matter of the type of instruction needed for trade related theory to be taught in the vocational schools for apprentices, became interested in another matter which was to have added importance in future years. Those of us who were concerned with the problem of competency of employees, were deeply conscious of the educational needs of the young men who could not have had the privilege of college courses, but who could cover much of the same ground in an evening school program, if such could be made available. There was nowhere such a program. Consequently, we devised a curriculum which high school graduates might pursue provided we could find the educational institutions willing and able to provide such a program, or parts of such a program. We first thought that we could accomplish this by getting the services of any institution of learning in the community that could offer any part of the curriculum. We organized ourselves into an Industrial Training Conference with appropriate letterhead.

The responsibility of being Chairman of the Industrial Training Conference was placed on me. The first thing we did was to write to each of the educational institutions in Milwaukee to determine what particular part of the proposed curriculum it could make available for our purposes. All the replies were negative, except that of the Milwaukee Vocational School, whose Director, Dr. R. L. Cooley, arranged for an appointment to discuss the possibility of providing for our needs. I, myself, presented the plan to Dr. Cooley. He later presented it to the Milwaukee Board of Vocational Education. At this point, it should be said that evening courses were carried on for adults at the request of potential students. The Continuation School[28] law made it mandatory for the Continuation School Board to offer particular evening courses if twelve or more persons petitioned for such a course. However, evening courses given were individual courses on what might be termed an atomistic basis. There was no organized correlation or sequence to the individual studies. They did not constitute a consistent program of sequential, progressing courses of study with which students could advance. What was needed was a program with courses of study to span a period of five years in which the student would get the high points of a College of Engineering course, although not given for academic credit. The Milwaukee Vocational Board, after due consideration, decided to allow the Industrial Training Conference to try out the program by using school facilities and selecting the teachers for the course and taking full responsibility for the operation of the program. The Board wanted us to try out the program on our own to see if

---

[28] The name previously established in the law, really the same as the Vocational School.

it would succeed before making it a facet of the Vocational School program. The Board was not disposed to risk an enterprise that might fail. The Vocational School as a new institution had yet to win more public support. Consequently, we went ahead, laid out the program, selected the teachers, and appointed one of our group to supervise the operation of the program.

The enterprise was a success from the start. At the end of two years of phenomenal success, the Vocational School took over the program which was designed the Evening Technical Course. Put in charge of the program at this point was William Patterson[29] of the Vocational School. As far as I can determine, this was the first program of this kind in the country. However, in subsequent years, this idea of evening sequential courses received wide approval and use especially after the return of veterans of World War II. This Evening Technical Course established in 1924 was expanded and later known as the Milwaukee Institute of Technology. Early in the year 1968 the title became officially known as "Milwaukee Area Technical College." While at first the courses were of an engineering nature, courses for students who had completed high school or had an equivalent education and have the ability to carry post-high school courses successfully are now offered through five divisions of instruction, namely, (1) business, (2) graphic and applied arts, (3) technical, (4) television, and (5) general education – junior college, that is. This institution is accredited by the North Central Association of Colleges and Secondary Schools for certain parts of the curriculum. It is also officially approved and accredited by the Wisconsin State Board of Vocational and Adult Education and is a member of the American Association of Junior Colleges and the American Council on Education.

I, myself, taught courses in the early years of this program,

---

[29] Mr. Patterson, as related elsewhere, was later the Director of the Bureau of Apprentice, Department of Labor.

among which were labor history, economics, industrial management and personnel administration; I continued until the exigencies of World War II made it necessary for me to give up this assignment. In 1952, the Milwaukee Board of Vocational and Adult Education gave me and my pioneer compatriots an honorary citation, publicly presented, as the founders of the Milwaukee Institute of Technology, now the Milwaukee Area Technical College.

In the summer of 1926, I decided to take my wife with our two young boys, 4 and 8 respectively, to visit my home and native land, which my wife had not yet seen. At some sacrifice, I persuaded my wife to stay abroad for the four seasons, since this experience would enhance the value of our future years together. I thought it was not enough to have a short visit; such would be insufficient to understand the conditioning factors of my first twenty years. During this period, the older boy (Nevin) was placed in a private boarding school in Hunstanton on the east coast of England. The younger boy (Norman) stayed with one of my sisters, who had a boy the same age. He attended a kindergarten in which my sister was a teacher. Meanwhile, my wife made her headquarters in the city of London with another of my sisters, and there arranged for several trips to the European continent, and then, in the season studied practically every dramatic performance on the London stage. This indeed was not an idle past-time; it took on the character of graduate study, since her major in college and in graduate work was speech and dramatics. In the meantime, I had returned at the end of summer and was back on my professional duties which enabled me to send the financial support necessary to enable my wife to enjoy her experience with some independence. Fortunately, since my family was abroad, I had plenty to occupy my mind. I was able to concentrate on my doctoral dissertation and to obtain my PhD degree from the University of Wisconsin.

During that academic year 1926 and 27, I was induced to write a book on apprenticeship which would be an elaboration of my PhD dissertation. This was to be edited for a vocational series. The book was published by McGraw-Hill in 1932. The Great Depression hurt the sale of the book. However, it was accepted as the one authoritative book on modern apprenticeship. This work I was to learn later was one of four books required for study in all the vocational teacher training programs in the country.

In the spring of 1927, my wife and children returned from abroad. We had appreciated the break from the strenuous social life of the early twenties, which prevailed in the growing suburbs of that day. It was a sort of "rebound" from the wartime atmosphere. The new families that were started following the war, and the coming of age of the great transportation phenomenon known as the automobile, caused the suburbs to expand and the home building boom to accelerate. Social activity was feverish.

Some of our friends invited us to join one of the new golf clubs being organized in the twenties. We voted against it. We preferred to take the potential golf club expenses and establish a summer home in the northern part of Wisconsin. Through neighbors, who owned some strategic shoreline, we purchased a lot on a "shoestring." There, 250 miles north of Milwaukee, we chopped a hole in the woods for the first unit, a twelve by twenty-four frame building with ten-foot studs (The money to obtain the building material came from the earnings of my wife, who that summer taught oral English to the students of the University of Wisconsin Labor School). This enterprise was another example of how my acquired building trade skills paid off. I built the first unit and all succeeding units myself.

We improved the premises each successive season with our vacation money, so that after thirty-five years, we have evolved a very comfortable summer home acquired without financial strain. This summer diversion is what an academic career calls for. There is a time when it is necessary to have privacy; time for philosophic contemplation, an opportunity to enhance health

considerations and enjoy "re-creation" for new academic responsibilities. Another factor of some importance was the fact that as
a victim of hay fever, there was complete relief in the northern
woods surrounded by the lakes.

At this time vacations were short. The first unit of this cot-
tage referred to was built in ten days of a two-week vacation.
The ninety days of summer did not materialize for me until the
thirties. Even then I used to think that I was too young in years
to justify such a vacation. However, I reasoned that one really
"has only what one lives." I desired a balanced life for myself
and family. Our two boys had a greater affection for the home
in the north than they had for the one in the city. They thrived
on boating and swimming and in the study of wildlife, a wonderful springboard for a potential scientist which Nevin ultimately
became.[30]

However, the summers spent in the woods did necessarily
place limits on one's annual income. However, as I told my students, there was a "psychic income," an increment of satisfaction, which in itself was worth all it cost.

Obviously, to live on a professor's salary in those days with
two homes to maintain, it was necessary to have simple tastes and
to obtain the advantages of high thinking to enjoy those things
which money could not buy. It was interesting to me to have a
man whose income was about three times as much as mine say,
"If I were wealthy, I would have a home up north." I myself was
not wealthy, measured by this world's goods, but wealthy in in-
tangibles. The building and engineering techniques required to
set up the lake establishment was what I possessed, or had acquired. Every aspect of the construction was performed by me
with what help the other members of the family could provide.
Carpentry, cabinet making, masonry, plumbing, electricity, heat-

---

[30] At the time of writing (1968), Head of the Department of Nutrition and Food
Science, Massachusetts Institute of Technology.

ing, sanitation, painting, tree felling, etc., etc., was by our own hands. All these tasks provided a challenge which was interesting and good exercise. I think this extended my life. It seems to me that many of my contemporaries have carried their obsession with their professional life beyond the realm of prudence. It is very easy to overevaluate one's contribution to contemporary society. Of course, one should do what one reasonably can to make a contribution to his day and generation but not to expect to reform mankind for all times. Each generation has to stand by itself. What may have seemed important yesterday may have no meaning tomorrow.

In other words, I think there should be a limit to one's sacrifices for professional achievement. Moreover, a man should not make his family sacrifice too much for his advancement, in what, in the last analysis, may not be too important anyway. It is not improbable that a person with an extended life at a moderate pace could achieve as much, or more, than one who lives strenuously for a shorter period. It is a sad experience to witness the passing of an able person of unripe age who had worked himself to death when he might have made a contribution for many more years.

In the fall semester of 1928, my services were deemed more valuable to the University as a full-time professor of economics and industrial relations. From then on my duties consisted of teaching economics to engineering students and personnel management to business administration students. At this time also it was necessary to relinquish my connection with the Kearney-Trecker Corporation. I had had an uncomfortable feeling trying to be an objective academic scholar while at the same time being more or less cramped in style by my association with a profit-making industrial concern, which naturally would expect my expressed ideas to coincide with those of industry. This is the same concern which caused me to give up my membership in a union. I had a strong feeling that a person who is teaching objectively the problems of our economic society cannot afford to be compromised by membership in some particular group with a particular slant with reference to the equities or inequities of the system.

The fall of 1929 witnessed the debacle of the stock market decline which proved the vanguard of the Great Depression. The Depression made the subject of economics not only popular but an obsession. It seemed that every philosopher or pseudo-philosopher who could get an audience had a cure for the Depression. This, of course, meant that a genuine student of economics with proper credentials was in demand as a speaker on specific aspects of the economy. Subjects on which it was my opportunity to present to many audiences included the gold standard, banking, inflation, international war debts, the devaluation of the dollar, and other like subjects. I was in great demand as a speaker at that time as a perusal of the local daily press of those days will document.

In the early thirties, the YMCA was conducting an annual conference at Lake Geneva, Wisconsin on the subject of human relations in industry. For the 1931 conference, I was approached and asked to take the major role in this conference. On three successive days, I was to make a presentation of a subject for one hour and then the conference was to be divided into groups to discuss the content of this presentation. I chose for my overall title the subject, "The Challenge of the Depression." It must be remembered that this was in 1931 before Franklin Roosevelt was nominated for the presidency of the United States. At this conference, I advocated unemployment insurance which was not as yet established anywhere in the United States. This was a delicate subject in some respects because industry then looked askance at any such scheme.

I had another strong conviction at that time, which I still hold, and that is that there can be no such thing as world peace without international trade and economic dealings between nations. This was a time when economic isolation seemed to be an American fetish and protective tariffs almost a "sacred cow." I used every opportunity of public discussion to point out how inimical to the United States and World Peace were the United States protective tariffs. Fortunately, by the time of this writing we have learned the lesson at least, in part, after two devastating wars with a colossal loss of life, which sadly enough took away many of our finest and most talented young men, including a son of my own.

In 1931, it was still not acceptable in business circles to project the institution of organized labor as an asset in an individualistic society. However, in the first day's lecture of the annual Conference on Human Relations in Industry, after reviewing labor history, I made the following observation:

> "The evolution of human relations in industry may be compared to the movement of a mighty river, the "father of waters." Into the movement of the master-stream and accelerating its pace are other tributary streams. The organized labor movement, which we have spoken about, may be likened as one of the convening forces that push forward the main waters, but it has not been the whole consideration.
>
> "It is in point to observe that when the statement is made to the effect that all personnel work has been established to avoid unionism, there is failure to understand the necessities of scientific management. It may be true that 'welfare work' may have been instituted to avoid the trade union. However, it is not fair to assume, as many do, that all personnel activity is directed against the union."[31]

In the third lecture, entitled "The Challenge of the Depres-

---

[31] Bulletin, Human Relations in Industry, 14th Annual Conference, Lake Geneva, 1931.

sion," I postulated the following considerations to set forth some of the more fundamental ways in which the challenge of the Depression could be met:

In the first place a society is not a mere collection of individuals. It is a functioning group. "It used to be thought that economic science would be a thing apart from other sciences, but now we know that a person cannot understand economics unless he knows something of the political background, the social conditions, the religious faiths, the ethical sense, and other aspects of the lives of people which form the center of interest in the social sciences."

In the second place, I pointed out the necessity for obtaining the facts. Many, many times in my experience have I discovered responsible people failing to get the facts—this, with reference to unemployment, obsolescence, etc. People are loath to embrace discomforting information; they are prone to ascribe social and economic maladjustments to be the fault of those who are victimized by them. As one employer told me at this time, "It is the employee's own fault if he is out of work, for he chose the wrong line of work."

A third consideration, which in 1931 was a tender spot, was the inequities in the distribution of the national product. This certainly received primary attention later with the "New Deal."

As a fourth consideration, I posed the necessity for adequate provision against industrial hazards, the hazards of unemployment, illness, and obsolescence. At the time the following statement in the lecture created a stir. "Uppermost in everybody's mind these days is the question of the hazard of unemployment . . . Unemployment insurance does not eliminate unemployment any more than fire insurance eliminates fires. It does, however, help to withstand its hardships . . . Individual employers cannot meet the situation alone, except the unusually large concerns. If unemployment is a necessary part of modern industrial civilization, then its price must be paid, which is, at a minimum, the maintenance of those out of work and in need. Insurance is better than charity." A final step which I presented was for more comprehensive vocational training and guidance.

The year following, Wisconsin passed the first unemployment compensation law authored by my former graduate school professor, John R. Commons. The law was first introduced as a bill in Wisconsin's 1921 Legislature. The first legislative hearing of this bill created quite a stir. I was privileged to attend this hearing myself. This "innovation" from the standpoint of employers created deep concern. At this first hearing, employer's representatives from the Wisconsin Manufacturing Association, the Milwaukee Metal Trades Association and the Association of Commerce filled a Parlor car on the morning train enroute for Madison. I, myself, was among the group as a member of the Milwaukee Metal Trades Association's Legislative Committee.

The above accounting is to point out the circumstances of the pre-New Deal economy – no provision for the unemployed, only the "poor house" for the aged indigent, no federal housing, collective bargaining unprotected, no restraint on court injunctions against union activity. We were still trying to rationalize a "laissez faire" economy.

One could go on only to emphasize how far we have traveled since the early thirties. We have now many built-in safeguards against cataclysmic depressions. The only sad thing about it is that the generations who are the beneficiaries are unable to appreciate the full significance of this social legislation of the thirties, and the efforts of the many socially minded and forward looking persons who worked with dedication to bring to pass these reforms.

In the Depression year of 1930 I had served on the Milwaukee County Committee on Unemployment. This was an interesting and informative experience but one of total frustration. The impact of the economic depression was national in character and beyond the ability of local public authority to find solutions.

In the spring of 1934, the Milwaukee County Board appointed a committee of fifteen, on which I served, to study the question of the consolidation of metropolitan functions, many of which are carried on by the respective municipalities in the area, something like, let's say, the library services, or the fire fighting services. The Metropolitan sewage commission function was a prototype of what might be considered the model. I, myself, served on a subcommittee of five which was appointed to meet with a similar committee representing the city of Milwaukee. The result of our efforts was a recommendation, subsequently adopted, that the parks of the various municipalities should be combined under the authority of a County Park Commission. This was the only positive action resulting from the whole committee. The time was not yet ripe for county consolidation of metropolitan functions. I should add that I served on this committee as a representative of Marquette University.

During the year of 1925, I became the first professor of Economics in the Marquette University Graduate School and was the chairman in 1925 of a small committee responsible for the first regular graduate school bulletin. On this committee with me was Father Frumveller, S. J. who subsequently left Marquette for Detroit. This was a time when the Milwaukee public school teachers were being pressed to get master's degrees, or at least to further their academic studies. This was encouraged as a means to obtain higher salaries. Consequently, during these Depression years, it was my pleasure to meet teachers in afternoon graduate classes.

As related elsewhere, the Wagner Labor Act was passed in June, 1935. Subsequently, there was great tension in employee-management relations. I was in on many labor disputes and served in many situations as an arbitrator. I was appalled at the evidence of human selfishness and lack of understanding on both sides. By 1937, the communists were infiltrating young people's groups in many directions. The American Youth Congress, a communist front organization, was going full blast. The whole industrial relations atmosphere was extremely disconcerting. As related in Chapter VII, I had served as Director of the Milwaukee Regional Labor Board.

I decided I needed a change. So with my wife's encouragement I took a summer trip to Europe and visited my 87-year old mother, and at the same time made a point of studying English industrial relations in London, Toynbee on Tees, Birmingham, Sheffield, etc. The contract in English labor relations with the experience in the United States convinced me that we had at that time much to learn and to experience before it could be said that American labor relations had matured.

I should relate that on my way to embark on the *Queen Mary* for Southampton, I called on my friend, William Patterson, the director of the Bureau of Apprenticeship, under the Secretary of Labor, Miss Frances Perkins. While visiting the Department of Labor, I obtained a courtesy letter from Miss Perkins, whom I had known when she was secretary for the New York Industrial Commission. We had participated in the same program at a National Conference of Labor Commissioners in Seattle, Washington, June 1920. The possession of this letter turned out to be extremely fortunate for me. When I was ready to board the ship in New York Harbor I was minus a passport, which I had left behind in Wauwatosa. My family was now in our summer home in Northern Wisconsin. I was flabbergasted. But while going over papers from my pocket hoping against hope that I might find the passport, a ship officer caught sight of the letter from Miss Perkins. He looked at me and said, "What are you doing with that letter from Miss Perkins?" I invited him to read it. Then he said, "We will let you in on the ship on the strength of that letter. If you can take a chance, so can we."

Of course, it is a serious thing not to have a passport, not so much when you go out of the country as when you want to return. I was quite relieved. I called Patterson in Washington who took my plight to the U.S. State Department.

Anyway I sailed without the passport, and then halfway across the Atlantic, I received a cablegram from the State Department advising me to get a duplicate passport from the American consul in either London or Southampton. On arriving at Southampton, I was paged on the ship as "Professor Scrimshaw" and was escorted off the ship, on instructions from the State Department. This enabled me to board the boat-train for London ahead of most other passengers. This was quite a thrill. It enhanced my pride in being a United States citizen.

While abroad I visited Denmark. I was greatly impressed by the Danes, a courteous people with a deep sense of humor and an appreciation for the welfare of others. I found their Tivoli, Copenhagen an unbelievably fine recreation institution which seemed to breathe the spirit of the people and provide superb entertainment for all classes of people at a minimum of expense, and which did not make obvious the commercial motivation. Strangely enough, as I write this, there is discussion in Milwaukee, Wisconsin with reference to the exploring of the idea of a Tivoli for this city. It remains to be seen, whether a Midwest city such as Milwaukee could emulate the Danes. Tivoli, Copenhagen was conceived in a less materialistic age and with a more articulate cultural background. If Milwaukee can make a cultural as well as financial success of such an institution, then it will indeed be evidence of progress.

In visiting Sweden, I was impressed with the revelation of modern architecture. It was difficult to one coming from the isolationist background of the United States to learn that we in the United States were not always ahead of the world in everything.

The most outstanding experiences of this 1937 European excursion was the ominous impression I had of the Paris International Exposition. The atmosphere was charged. On the Exposition grounds the building housing the German contribution displayed a large swastika opposite the Soviet building which displayed similarly the hammer and sickle. These two manifestations of double jeopardy for Western civilization was frightening. The international cooperative spirit which is the *sine qua non* of such an exposition was difficult to find if not completely missing. In fact by midsummer the United States exhibit was incomplete and I was told afterwards that it never was really finished.

All over Paris there were signs of *Propriété à vendre* (property for sale). Hotel managers showed apprehension for the future and expressed the feeling that there was trouble in the air. Two subversive movements were afoot – one the threat of Russian Communism, and the other the rising menace of Nazi Germany. It can easily be understood how glad I was to be returning home to take up the challenge of the Fall semester to carry on the life of a professor.

In September, I returned to the University reinforced in my capacity to conduct classes in economics and industrial relations. However, so far as my College of Engineering faculty associates were concerned, it was revealing to relate that the first day after my return, while we were gathered around the table for lunch, I was given an insight that I never forgot. I expected those present to be interested in my travel experiences. At first they appeared to be, and some questions were asked which gave me the opportunity to make a few observations. This lasted about ten minutes. I was about to tell some interesting revelations when, all of a sudden, the conversation switched to football. From that moment onward, no one of the group showed any further interest in what was going on abroad. This experience revealed the intellectual insularity of the American mind before World War II. It reflected the isolationist position of the United States in matters both political and economic.

In 1938 as an aftermath of my experience with the consultation group of the U. S. Department of Labor, Bureau of Apprenticeship referred to in Chapter V, I was invited to join the summer session of the Department of Vocational teacher training at the Oklahoma Agricultural and Mechanical College in Norman,

Oklahoma. The Federal government had appropriated money to promote apprenticeship in the states.

I was to conduct a class in industrial relations and go out into the cities of the state to promote apprenticeship, an undertaking I was well qualified to pursue.

The purpose of this was to persuade the state to pass an apprenticeship law such as was proposed by the Department of Labor. The Federal government provided some subsidy to the state to meet the expenses involved.

My students were vocational school and industrial arts teachers. The experience was stimulating and enjoyable but the climate was one of oppressive heat, the like of which, so far in my life, I had never experienced. One morning I was asked to forego a class session in order that the students could assemble with other classes to see an industrial film. I was disappointed to lose this class session for a matter which I though would be of little consequence. I was agreeably surprised when the movie commenced, to find that it was a film in which I myself had the initial part by the way of comment on the merits of the Nunn-Bush 52-checks-a-week plan, instituted in 1935 and prompted by the unemployment conditions of the Depression. This was accompanied by pictures of Marquette University buildings forming a background of appropriate setting. It was strange that I should meet myself in action in a southwestern state so far from home. Of course, whoever made the arrangements knew nothing of my being on the campus.

I was engaged for a similar second summer session in 1939, presenting the problems of apprenticeship training and personnel administration.

Chapter IX

RETROSPECT

Mankind learns only the hard way.

Man exists within the mechanism of organized society. Organized society, however, seems at times to cramp the style of the individual. Therefore, man is perpetually seeking to change the arrangement of organized society with the belief that such changes will enhance the individual's life's goal, or realization of what is contemplated when using the expression "pursuit of happiness." These changes or social modifications run the gamut of all phases of human behavior. One might conclude that the dissatisfaction with the "status quo" and the movement to provide changes is a part of the process involved in pursuit of that happiness which is indefinable, illusory and unrealized.

These phases of human behavior lend themselves to many distinct disciplines or classified fields of knowledge, which although they may appear to lead in different directions, are nevertheless integrated as they center around man himself.

As one time the emphasis may be on political measures, another time it might be on aspects of economic organization, then again, it might be on a matter of health and morals, etc. It is rarely understood how many facets of human experience affect human behavior at any period of time.

Human relations, one way or another are affected by all the

elements involved in the functioning of our social order. To convey the full import of the above observation, I will quote from a manual I prepared for students of personnel management during the years of the Great Depression.

> Some of the outside considerations which affect human behavior are the following: protective tariffs, monetary systems, political situations such as revolutions, elections and the like, strikes, lockouts, legislation, court decisions, new inventions, new discoveries, new modes of communication, new means of transportation, wars, "acts of God" (earthquakes, floods, droughts, hurricanes, typhoons, plagues, etc.), trade agreements, mergers, international treaties, credit situations, business booms and depressions, custom and fashion, discoveries of new markets, transportation rates, immigration, racial conflicts, and although less obvious but very profoundly, philosophies of life.

One learns from long experience that there is no "royal road." From time to time great issues arise which seem to promise a solution of a particular social problem but they rarely ever meet expectations. During this century social reform has been a major concern, and because of the rapid changes in science and technology and the extensive development of general education, there evolved many issues upon which it seemed that the welfare of society depended. However, that "welfare" no matter how conceived is apparently never fully realized. While it is true that reforms may bring desirable changes, it does not follow that the individuals in the social order are convinced that their welfare has been achieved. Many so-called reforms are only palliatives acting like drugs, which may ease a particular symptom but bring side effects which introduce other problems. Moreover, satisfaction is a condition of the mind, a very subjective phenomenon.

As one looks back over this century, he realizes that the

much-heralded reforms have not removed human discontent. People today in many ways seem more unhappy and restless than the people of 50 years ago.

Thereby hangs a tale. Americans are prone to go to extremes. They push hard for changes and usually overestimate advantages to accrue from what may be considered essential reforms.

It is easy to cite some of the major issues and reforms since the beginning of the century and to point out both their positive and negative aspects. These show in retrospect the limitations of legislative pressures on human behavior.

World War I, we believed, was fought, in the words of Woodrow Wilson, "to make the world safe for democracy." However, that was not the result. Instead it laid the seeds of the Second World War and made possible the Communist empire. It destroyed a generation of potential British leaders and drained Britain's financial resources from which it never recovered.

In the United States, the consequences of the war were not so grave. It brought greater unity of feeling in the nation, and a realization of our great strength. Aside from the acceleration of science and technology, World War I caused the induction of more women into industrial production for the war effort. The consequences of this fact hastened the development of better working conditions in the factories. This was necessary to accommodate the women and to induce them to accept employment in the war industries. The employment of women helped to focus attention on the drive for Women's Suffrage. Women's Suffrage was a very persistent movement – heralded as a major political reform. Many thought that it would be the sure way to achieve lasting peace, for women are the mothers of the race and opposed to the destruction of their offspring in war. Finally both in Britain and the United States, women's suffrage was achieved. In this country it came with the adoption of the XIX amendment to the U. S. Constitution. However, in retrospect it is obvious that the direct advantages were not as astounding as advocates had claimed.

The advantages of women's suffrage to our society, it appears to me, were indirect rather than direct. Suffrage brought women more significantly into the socio-economic fabric. Women have brought about political enlightenment to large areas of our citizenship that hitherto were oblivious to what was going on in men's political world.

This new status for women in our society has had an incalculable effect on our whole existence. This was born in upon me as a Training Consultant in the process of training 2,000 women for specific operations requiring extensive skill, in a large defense industry during World War II.

The success of that war effort owed much to the remarkable contribution of the women of all economic strata, and that obviously is an understatement.

As a student in the years before World War I, I was intrigued with some other dominant issues of the day. Some of these issues inevitably came in focus through inter-collegiate debates. One of these issues was the question of establishing Postal Savings Banks to accommodate European immigrants who were suspicious of American banks, which up to that time, had a not very assuring record of stability. Periodically through our history, with the phenomenon of the business cycle, there were always a series of bank failures with devastating results.

In due time Congress did pass a statute providing for postal savings. This institution was used by the first generation of immigrants who were accustomed to it in their homelands, but their offspring, native-born Americans, had little interest in following this practice for themselves. The postal savings bank system was abolished in the '60's.

Speaking of banks brings forth the issue of "financial reform." In the year 1907 there occurred a financial panic due to the inelasticity of the currency. It seemed that in the fall of the year when it was necessary to have money to move the crops in the West, there was a shortage of currency in the East. Currency was then based on gold. That made it inelastic. Many times banks in the East could not accommodate all their customers, especially if rumors started a "run on the bank." At such times there would be an economic collapse, financial losses for many people, and forced unemployment.

Many manipulators of the money market could profit unduly under these circumstances, and they did.

After 1907 the demand for reform of the currency was persistent. Finally, by 1913 Congress passed the Federal Reserve Act. While a graduate student at the University of Wisconsin where our professor of banking had helped to write the law, we received a batch of the first copies of this new law. Soon thereafter I found myself assigned from time to time to present an explanation of the Federal Reserve System to interested groups.

This Federal Reserve Act established twelve banks for the whole country to serve as Banker's Banks. In effect these are banks to provide credit wholesale to the member banks of the system, who then provide credit to their customers retail. On top of this, the law required only 40 per cent of gold reserve for the dollar where previously 100 per cent was required. The remaining security was commercial paper backed by forms of wealth (other than gold). This was a brand new concept. Some years later the amount of gold reserve was reduced to 25 per cent. At the time of writing, serious consideration is being given to the question of eliminating the requirement for a gold reserve for the currency.

This reform of the currency came just in time to finance the First World War. It has been postulated by banking authorities that we could not have financed World War I without such a mechanism as the Federal Reserve System.

World War I, of course, did not make the world safe for democracy. It did, however, usher in a new era of astounding change, much of which, of course, could be termed progress.

Up until 1914 it could be said that we in the United States

were still in an agricultural economy. The farmers constituted a political factor that, for the most part, dominated national elections. The individualism characteristic of the independent farmer was a highly valued attribute of life.

The immigrant, too, had to fight his way as an individual. This fact accounted for many celebrated American success careers of "self-made men." Whatever else were the merits of rugged individualism, there is no doubt that it seemed to embody the principle of "every man for himself and the devil take the hindmost." What to some individuals was the pursuit of happiness could impair the happiness of others.

An important issue of the early years of this century was the regulation of immigration. This has been implied previously in this work. It is mentioned now, in retrospect, to point out that however overwhelming an issue can be, sooner or later it recedes in importance, while another social problem becomes the pervading issue of the day.

Exploitation of immigrants by American industry brought into focus the shocking condition of industrial employees in our factories and mines. The supply of labor was greater than the demand. There was always somebody ready to take the other fellow's job, so individual workers were in no position to bargain for more favorable working conditions.

Although during the First World War, immigration was practically shut off, following the war, the country was not disposed to tolerate again unregulated immigration. During the war there had been encountered problems with respect to the loyalty of some ethnic groups, and it was realized that European immigration had been too great to achieve proper assimilation. As a consequence the problem of Americanization became a big issue. As pointed out in Chapter V, this matter of Americanization was comprehended in the Vocational Education movement, aided and abetted, of course, by the passage of the restrictive 1920 Immigration Quota Act which reduced immigration, figuratively speaking, to a trickle. Now the prosperity of the '20's, after stemming the supply of immigrant labor, seemed to promise opportunity for organized labor to come into its own. However, that was not yet to be.

The phenomenon of the First World War had so accelerated industrial technology as to bring about an increase in the national productivity. Labor, of course, shared some of this productivity increase and profited from the decline in prices of goods and services brought about by competition and improved technology. Consequently, labor made little headway in organization. Labor leaders had a hard time to sell unionism. Individualism was still considered a high virtue, and on top of all that, there was the sinister nation-wide propaganda to promote the so-called "open shop," or the American plan.

Organized employers, such as the National Metal Trades Association, and the National Manufacturer's Association, State Manufacturer's Associations and the like, spent great sums of money to propagate the so-called "open shop." The industrial literature of the time attempted to extol industrial achievement of non-union shops. The post-World War I economic troubles of Great Britain were attributed by American industrialists to the existence of unions. It was said that the United States was prosperous by virtue of the fact that it was not so highly unionized. So went the propaganda until its futility was manifest after the stock market crash of 1929 which ushered in a new era. As discussed in Chapter VII, the New Deal embraced organized labor, consequently propaganda for the open shop was soon dead and buried.

Another of the early political issues was the question of the popular election of senators. This it was claimed would eliminate the political corruption generated by the method of electing U. S. senators by state legislatures or by "stacked" conventions. This was a subject widely and warmly discussed as though its attainment would be the last word in representative democracy.

Consequently by 1913 a new amendment to the United States Constitution was adopted. This XVII amendment provided that U. S. senators should be chosen by the popular vote of the electorate. The popular election of U. S. senators, whatever it merits, did not necessarily produce higher type senators or for that matter, eliminate corruption, or necessarily express the popular will.

As a matter of hindsight, let us take a look at the question of prohibition. In the years before World War I, the Anti-Saloon league carried on such a vigorous and sustained campaign over many years as to succeed in impressing the public and the lawmakers to adopt in 1918 an amendment to the Constitution of the United States to make illegal the manufacture, transportation and sale of intoxicating liquor. This became the XVIII amendment. This, it was claimed, would eliminate the "devil's half acre" of our cities, get rid of prostitution and guarantee a sober and well-behaved citizenry, etc. President Hoover called it a "noble experiment," a strange experiment it was for a nation which came into being by virtue of the desire of the people for personal freedom.

Prohibition did not solve the problems of alcoholism or social immorality, but it did unwittingly develop an era of lawlessness and gangsterism, the fruits of which even over a half century after the repeal of the prohibition, are still with us. Moreover, it was a moot question as to whether this reform measure really reflected the popular will. If it did, it manifestly showed how fickle is the popular will. By the year 1933 this prohibition amendment was repealed presumably to satisfy the same popular will.

Early in the century on the state level a reform proposal, widely discussed, was the question of the Initiative and Referendum. It was believed that elected representatives are prone to ignore the will of the people – that they do not meet their responsibilities on legislating for the public needs. It was thought that there should be means to force legislation when there was public demand, if the elected representatives of the people failed to act. This indeed was hailed as the crowning solution to ineffective government. In due time in many states the Initiative and Referendum was legalized, an action which seemed to be the "last word" in legislative reform. Now it was said, the lawmakers must really act for the people, or the people will propose legislation by petition and if necessary adopt the measure in question by a popular referendum. Needless to say, not even this measure solved all the lawmaking problems or omissions. Occasionally the initiative has been used, and the referendum a little more, because the latter allows politicians to get "off the hook" on controversial questions. Politicians can "pass the buck" when they should, really, on their own, accept their responsibility to make decisions in the light of the public good.

In spite of all these reforms there was still wide areas of dissatisfaction. For one thing, organized labor was complaining about the use of injunctions in labor disputes which made it virtually impossible for labor to organize. This problem was a matter of public debate for a long generation.

The Bull Moose third party in the general election of 1912 was committed in its platform to curb injunctions in labor dispute. However, the statute which finally accomplished this much extolled reform was not passed until the year 1932.

This piece of legislation enacted just before the New Deal, as implied in the discussion in Chapter VII, opened a "Pandora's box," and precipitated labor relations problems, still unresolved. Later came the Wagner Act of 1935 which was presumed to clarify the total labor problem. However, the extraordinary power bequeathed to labor was in the eyes of large segments of the public a cure worse than the disease. After twelve years of trial, Congress passed the Taft-Hartley Act to make the unions and their leaders responsible. This is presented in detail in Chapter VII. The whole experience points up the fact that you cannot legislate mutual confidence. Legislation cannot determine the character of labor leaders. Laws cannot establish good will between unions and management, nor insure honesty on the part of the parties in dispute. This was shown by the necessity for the passage of the Lundrum-Griffin Act of 1938 mentioned in Chapter VII. The end is not yet. Final solutions are not attainable by laws but by self-discipline in the practice of good citizenship. Mankind learns the hard way and I am inclined to believe that it learns only the hard way.

A more recent issue is that of civil rights. Legislation to guarantee civil justice and equality before the law is a laudable achievement. However, legislation does not and cannot force desirable relationships in the social realm. Racial prejudice is in the minds of men. It is in the realm of education to eliminate bias and intolerance. These mental aberrations, if we can call them such, are not eliminated by government fiat, but by the will to understand and to live up to the Golden Rule, which we honor in the breech rather than in the observance. As a sideline observer, at this stage, it is of interest to see that each legislative enactment to achieve civil rights brings forth new problems, as does each court decision, pro or con.

The coming generations will find racial integration an arduous road, because it seems that, as I have observed before, mankind learns only the hard way.

Let me present another issue to prove the point made in the preceding paragraph. That issue is the subject of American Protective Tariff. During my active years, the question of protective tariffs was one of the great economic questions.

Protectionism in the United States started out as a plan to encourage infant industries. It later became an instrument of monopoly. As a debtor nation, there was some logic in protecting American industry against foreign competition. However the experiences in the years of the First World War showed that our situation had changed. We were no longer a debtor nation. Although prior to the World War 1914-1918 we were in debt to Europe to the tune of $4,000,000,000, it turned out at the funding of the European allied war debt in 1925 that Europe owed us $24,000,000,000. We were now a creditor nation but we still pursued the policy of a debtor nation. We demanded that the European nations pay the war debt, which sounds fair enough. However, during the same period of time, namely, in 1922 (that is, after the armistice), and in 1932, we raised the tariff on imports which in effect made it impossible for European nations to sell goods to the U.S. to enable them to obtain dollars to retire the debt.

Some international economists insisted that it would be in the economic interests of all the nations involved to cancel the war debts, and start fresh. American politicians could not seem to grasp the point. In a public discussion with a former governor of Wisconsin, I tried to point out that the debt could not be paid, but still the retort from him, a presumably intelligent political leader, was, "Our people won't stand for a cancellation of the war debts. They (meaning our war-time allies) borrowed the money and they must repay." Actually our war allies took war materials in a common effort. The war was fought with men, tanks, guns, ships, etc., but not with gold itself or with dollars.

At any rate, soon after the funding of the allied war debts in 1925 it became impossible for the debtors to continue payments on the debt as projected in the settlement plan.

Nations defaulted and matters had to drift. But in spite of it all, the U. S. passed the second post-war high tariff bill changing the rules from what they were at the time the debt was contracted. Two thousand economist members of the American Economics Association, including myself, signed a petition asking President Hoover to veto the Smoot-Hawley Tariff Act of 1932 since it was inimical to the economic interests of the U.S. No doubt the president was compromised because he signed the bill into law.

It was apparent that things were moving from bad to worse. A world wide economic depression was in the being. A new war became a threat and later a reality. We found ourselves pouring out lives and treasure to prevent a Nazi takeover. Now after the conclusion of the war we found it necessary to extend aid all around the world. How trivial seems the World War I debt of $24 billion in comparison with the huge price we had to pay in lives and treasure in the second world war, and since. At least we learned that protectionism is not the way to world peace. Free international trade is the key to peace. People don't want to fight those with whom they trade.

In the preceding pages I have pointed out some of the pros and cons of efforts to improve our industrial society with emphasis on the fact that as a people, or as a nation, we learn only the hard way. In other words, experience is our teacher and many times that comes at a pretty high price.

Some of our mistakes arise from the fact that in our subconscious we think too much of ourselves as a static society, when in reality we know there is no such thing in the modern world, if there ever was. Thinking of our social order in terms of something fixed we tend to think that specific measures of reform will accomplish a given result.

A survey of history will reveal the fact that in common language "nothing stays out." If, for example, it seems ominous that the Communists appear to be taking over the world, it is well to assure ourselves that things will change. New generations evolve deviations from the older generation. Fetishes of yesterday may be ignored tomorrow. It seems nothing we do can be guaranteed to be permanent. The only permanent things are intangible. We speak of the "eternal verities." They are in the spirit of man, love, kindness, charity, etc. In the material realm changes for good or ill are woven into the fabric of the universe. It is this phenomenon of change which can give hope that matters may improve in the tomorrows.

We sometimes get the query, "Do you think the world is getting better?" Although we can speculate that the material "world" gets better, however it is not at all certain that human nature gets better. When we read of the human problems of ancient Greece and the recital of human problems revealed by the lawgivers such as Lycurgus in 500 years B.C. and compare them to the problems of today, it is hard to believe that human beings have become better with the passage of time. The outcrop of barbarism which has shown itself in this twentieth century has accentuated the pessimistic view of human nature.

During this century we have passed many statutes on the state level designed to avoid the exploitation of employees, consumers and citizens generally. However, these enactments are never without limitations, or negative aspects. They never quite accomplish the results anticipated by the promoter of the law. The reason for this is inherent in human nature. Since we pride ourselves that our government is one of "laws," we are too prone to conclude that every social and economic problem can be solved when we carry out the idea in the slogan so often heard, "There ought to be a law." It seems simple. However, after a particular law is brought into being, questions arise with reference to its application in specific instances. Perhaps it conflicts with the enforcement of other laws, or may contravene the guarantee of the Constitution – our fundamental law. The courts have to resolve the issues that arise. As a consequence this process, known as "Judicial Review," results in some emasculation of the law as written. It is a matter of record that lawmakers can legislate reform, but the piece of legislation, after court review, is not the precise law that the legislators presumed it would be.

Another factor which is a limitation on protective labor laws is the negative element which arises out of the fact that people are involved. People are human, and human beings respond like human beings. For example, the Workmen's Compensation law which provides for compensation for loss of earnings due to injury may reveal as a by-product what is known as "malingering." Some individual employees feign disability when in reality they have none, or claim a greater degree of disability than actually exists. For the employers the law may cause them to require strict pre-employment physical examinations resulting in depriving some potential employees who would otherwise be satisfactory workers.

Another similar example is that of Unemployment Compensation. The positive aspects of the law are manifestly desirable, but here too there ensues some degree of malingering. When individuals are paid a high percentage of earnings over an extended period, they may feel, "Why work?" Another side effect is that it is difficult for John Q. Citizen to hire intermittent or part-time workers.

General education must, of course, be adapted to the needs of a dynamic society. Speaking in figurative language there are educators on the "right," educators on the "left," and some in the middle of the road. The extreme right want to maintain the "status quo," and follow tradition. Those on the extreme left continually seek changes, as manifested by those who so assiduously worked for "progressive education" which many of us thought brought irreparable damage to a whole generation, because of the slackening of the elements of personal discipline. On the other side were those who would have the schools use the nineteenth century Guffy readers in the third quarter of the twentieth. It is unfortunate that political ideology does reach into the area of educational philosophy.

Higher education has been less affected by political ideology but has been subject, in particular situations, to the pressures of *economic* philosophy. University boards of trustees or regents may reflect through some of its members a particular obsession concerning certain types of educational activities, especially those which might seem to threaten certain vested interests. On the whole, however, our universities have had an opportunity to blaze their own trail.

College education has been the great American dream. For a young nation we have had an incredible development of higher education. The children of the second and third generations of our late nineteenth century immigration have been pressured into attending college. Many times desire for status more than the thirst for knowledge accounts for the passion for a college degree on the part of parents for their offspring and children for their parents. Of course this applies for both the privileged and the unprivileged.

It seems to me as a person brought up in the "old world," that this new nation has achieved incomparable success in furnishing higher education on a democratic basis. It has been a by-product of our dedication to democracy. Higher education in the older countries in the past has been for the benefit of the leisure classes, but in this country it has taken on a very practical character, namely to help youth to acquire the abilities to "pull their weight in the boat," by earning a living. Consequently, much of the criticism aimed at college and university education is due to the fact that we strive to make available higher education to all who seek it. However, the mistake has been made on the supposition that all can make a profit by taking advantage of the same "educational diet."

In a normal class of undergraduate students it is pitiful at times to recognize on the part of some of the members of the class a complete lack of interest and comprehension. It is certain that not all students can have the same intellectual interests or activities. The situation calls for the diversification of educational institutions and programs. It is not defensible to insist that all young people should go to college. However, it is important that all should be given an opportunity to acquire advanced knowledge up to their capacity in the area in which they are interested. There is no justification for thinking the same educational process should or could fit everybody.

Of course, some part of our problem is in the idea of seeking status. Parents sometimes break the hearts of their offspring by insisting that they go to college when they might become excellent mechanics, business operators, and potentially prosperous entrepreneurs.

The American practice in the universities of trying to grade students A, B, C, D, E seems to me to be undignified. Students will challenge the professor's judgment in borderline situations. Well they might. The professor's standards themselves are not void of subjective elements. It seems we want an easy mechanistic way to classify students. I maintain the classification is too arbitrary. I think the European system of pass or fail would be better. The exceptional student could pass with honors.

Of course, certain standards must be maintained. As a friend of mine puts it, "If I am going to have a doctor operate on me, I want to know that he is competent."

The roots of our American educational commitment go back as far as the year 1825. This I have referred to in Chapter V.

The rationale for different types of curricula must be determined by society's needs, and student potential. I do not think that in a free enterprise economy schools should tailor their curricula for industrial and business needs at the expense of broader education. Specific training skills industry must provide for itself. In other words the students must be educated (I don't mean trained) for the benefit of the society as a whole, but with a view to functioning in an industrial society in the technological age. Sometimes this may come close to training for industry, especially if industry gives financial support. It is important however that the first consideration is for man in society, and after that the matter of fitting into a particular subsidiary economic sphere. Economic activity, with the short work week, takes less than a third of an adult's life in his working years. He has the promise of a long retirement when he is completely on his own. There are cultural needs to be recognized and developed.

While in retrospect on the subject of education, I would like to touch on a matter which in my judgment has been an academic headache and that is the undue emphasis on research at the expense of good teaching. The requirements, especially of undergraduate professors to carry on research with the principal "publish or perish" seems to me very short-sighted. A professor may be an excellent teacher who can research the minds of his students and give counsel of inestimable value to them for a lifetime, but who may have very little time, inclination or ability to turn out research papers. I am not referring to professors in the graduate schools, although even there a professor might achieve more, sometimes, helping and inspiring his students to do their research rather than exploiting them for his own.

In my experience I have known good teachers, underpaid, underequipped, and with heavy teaching loads, perennially harassed because of the lack of research. It goes something like this: "You expect a raise in salary? What research have you done?" Not a question of how good a teacher you are, or how beneficial is your influence on students and to what extent are they motivated and inspired by you. I have known "research" professors who are abominable teachers.

On the other hand, I have been fortunate to have had professors who were excellent instructors and inspiring educators who have ministered to the minds of many generations of students and who were so wrapped up in the process of giving their students a good academic start in life that they had no time for the proverbial individual research, which so often can turn out to be of such little consequence. My undergraduate professors in economics, biology, geology and philosophy were such men. They will be remembered not for their research projects but for what they did for their students. We need more educators like them.

It seems to me a crime to sell short the excellent teacher because he is not turning out publications. Not all teachers are good researchers, and good researchers are not necessarily good teachers.

Epilogue

So this is my story. It began with an apprenticeship as a master bricklayer in Lincolnshire, England completed at the age of 16, then emigration to America to pursue a college education. Having a trade enabled me to work my way through college and graduate school. Graduate studies in labor economics, my own apprenticeship experience, and a pending doctors thesis on apprenticeship led to my appointment by the Wisconsin legislature as the first state supervisor of apprenticeship in the United States to administer the first apprenticeship law.

My further career was determined when I accepted an appointment at Marquette University in Milwaukee, Wisconsin to set up a cooperative engineering program. As I have described, the many large manufacturing companies then thriving in Milwaukee were short of skilled labor due to changes in immigration regulations. The program made it economically possible for the American-born children of prior immigrants to fill skilled jobs in local industry. For me, it has led to a richly rewarding life devoted to labor economics.

Chronology

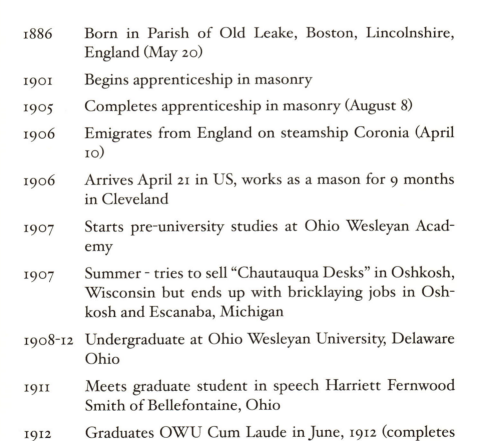

1886   Born in Parish of Old Leake, Boston, Lincolnshire, England (May 20)

1901   Begins apprenticeship in masonry

1905   Completes apprenticeship in masonry (August 8)

1906   Emigrates from England on steamship Coronia (April 10)

1906   Arrives April 21 in US, works as a mason for 9 months in Cleveland

1907   Starts pre-university studies at Ohio Wesleyan Academy

1907   Summer - tries to sell "Chautauqua Desks" in Oshkosh, Wisconsin but ends up with bricklaying jobs in Oshkosh and Escanaba, Michigan

1908-12 Undergraduate at Ohio Wesleyan University, Delaware Ohio

1911   Meets graduate student in speech Harriett Fernwood Smith of Bellefontaine, Ohio

1912   Graduates OWU Cum Laude in June, 1912 (completes high school and college in 4 2/3 years)

1912-15   Graduate student in economics at University of Wisconsin at Madison

1912-13   Assistant instructor in Transportation and Public Utilities

1915   Fellowship with the Industrial Commission of Wisconsin

1915-20   First administrator of Wisconsin's new apprenticeship system

1916   Marries Harriett Fernwood Smith (December 29)

1918   Birth of Nevin Stewart Scrimshaw (January 20)

1919   Builds own home in Madison, Wisconsin, with three fireplaces

1922   Birth of Norman Gilliat Scrimshaw

1922   Completes survey of opportunities for handicapped workers in Wisconsin State Board of Vocational Education

1922   Begins 32-year career as Professor of Economics and Industrial Relations, Marquette University, Milwaukee, Wisconsin

1922   Moves to Wauwatosa, Wisconsin

1920-28   Director of Personnel for Kearney and Trecker Corp. (part-time)

1925-26   Family trip to England

1926   Receives PhD in economics from University of Wisconsin; thesis title is "Principles of Apprenticeship Administration"

1927   Begins construction of summer home near Three Lakes, Wisconsin

1934   Appointed Associate Director of Chicago Regional

Labor Board, then Director of Milwaukee Regional Labor Board

1937 Conducts special investigation on labor relations in Great Britain

1944 Son Norman killed in France with General Patton's army (August 18)

1954 Retires from full-time academic duties at Marquette but continues to teach courses in labor relations and labor legislation

1968 Completes his autobiography

1973 Dies at age 86 (April 18)

Publications

Bricklaying in Modern Practice (New York: The MacMillan Company, 1920)

Apprenticeship: Principles, Relationships and Problems (New York: McGraw Hill Co., 1932.)